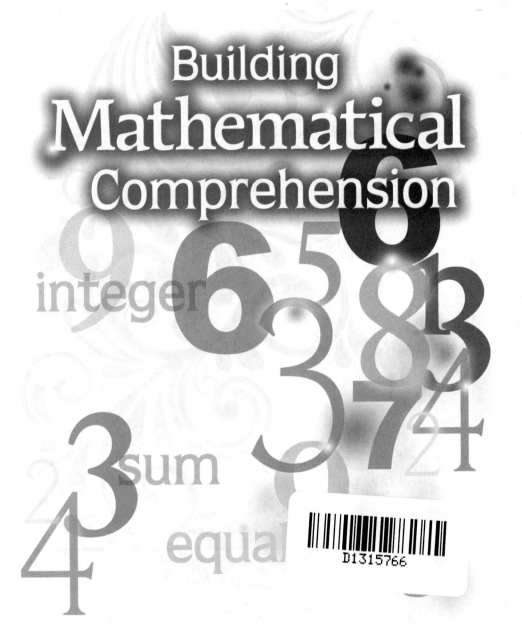

Building Mathematical Comprehension

Author
Laney Sammons

Foreword
Ruth Harbin Miles

SHELL EDUCATION

Publishing Credits

Dona Herweck Rice, *Editor-in-Chief*; Lee Aucoin, *Creative Director*;
Don Tran, *Print Production Manager*; Timothy J. Bradley, *Illustration Manager*;
Sara Johnson, M.S. Ed., *Senior Editor*; Hillary Wolfe, *Editor*; Juan Chavolla, *Cover Designer*;
Corinne Burton, M.A. Ed., *Publisher*

Shell Education

5301 Oceanus Drive
Huntington Beach, CA 92649-1030
http://www.shelleducation.com
ISBN 978-1-4258-0789-4
©2011 Shell Educational Publishing, Inc.

Table of Contents

Foreword

Over the past three decades, local, state, and national studies point out glaring deficiencies in mathematics instruction and call for changes to build greater comprehension and literacy in mathematics for all students. This publication addresses the need for and importance of increasing mathematics comprehension at all levels.

The author has included an analysis of the subject of comprehension of mathematics in the broadest sense. The essential elements are laid out in 10 chapters, each of which describes the strategies necessary for building mathematics comprehension for all learners. Connections are described and explained for readers.

One significant feature of this book is the recognition and understanding of the items and concepts included in the teaching of mathematical vocabulary. Another interesting focus is a section on inferences and predictions. The importance of visualizing mathematical ideas is stressed and suggestions on how to determine their importances are provided. A highlight of the book are the chapter Snapshots which provide the reader with a brief overview and analytical statement of what is to be learned from digesting the contents of the chapter. It serves as a study guide and assists in understanding the key points in the chapter. The ultimate outcome of a careful study of the subject matter should provide increasing comprehension as it is built up chapter by chapter.

Building Mathematical Comprehension provides a step-by-step guide and will become a valuable handbook for teachers in the field. The book is, in a very real sense, a pioneering effort to bring clarity to the subject of mathematical comprehension. In this respect, it is timely!

There are several unique features of the book that will be welcomed by teachers. Among these are: the seven comprehension strategies found in Chapter 1; the synthesizing information found in Chapter 8; and the use of questions for increasing student understanding found in Chapter 4. If there is a theme for this book, it would be called *connections* which are pointed out time after time for the attention of the readers.

The book contains up-to-date foundational research that should be very useful to mathematics teachers. This volume on the subject of building mathematics comprehension is a great contribution to the field of education and particularly mathematics education.

I think readers will find this book possesses utility and affords assistance to all mathematics teachers and that they will be amply rewarded for the application of the suggestion in this work. Coaches and supervisors will welcome this new tool for educators. It fills a gap that has long impeded the evaluation of teaching activities in mathematics. It should enhance the accurate reporting of results and lead to greater achievement on the part of mathematics teachers. Of course, the ultimate beneficiaries will be the students who will grasp the significance of mathematics concepts to a greater degree than ever before. In this sense, the profession is moving forward.

—Ruth Harbin Miles
Past NCSM President
Mathematics Educator
Mary Baldwin College
Staunton, Virginia

Acknowledgements

Just as creating classroom mathematical communities support the learning of our students, I receive support from a community composed of family, friends, educators, and editors. I can truly vouch for the benefits of being a part of such a community.

Thank you to members of the Yahoo Guided Math group and to the teachers I meet as I visit schools throughout the country. My learning continues and extends with every contact, suggestion, and question. Your enthusiasm and ideas inspire me!

I'd like to express my appreciation to Wendy Hamm, a good friend, an excellent instructional coach, and a fantastic photographer, for allowing her photographs to be included in this book. My heartfelt thanks, as well, to my good friends, Queenie Brost and Maggie Glennon. Their insights and perspectives guide me as I write.

My love and thanks to my family. Their ongoing support makes anything possible. My children and their families continue to check on my progress and boost my spirits. Checking in with my three grandchildren—Ash, Griff, and Sadie—is a constant reminder of the value of mathematics education.

By now, I am sure my husband is getting weary of my periodic absorption in writing. It is not easy to take care of all the household duties, not to mention emotional needs of someone who is day in and day out involved in writing a book. Thank you, Jack, for your incredible patience, support, and love. Who would have thought when we married thirty-nine years ago that this is what we would be doing?

And, I extend my gratitude to my editors at Shell Education, Sara Johnson and Hillary Wolfe. I value the working and personal relationships we have developed over the past few years.

—Laney

Preface

Good Teaching Is Good Teaching

In many ways, those who teach both reading and math have an advantage. Many of us never recognize this advantage, often feeling competent as reading teachers, but then struggling with mathematics instruction. This is puzzling because the demands of teaching each of these subject areas are similar.

As a classroom teacher, I was responsible for teaching all subject areas—with an emphasis on reading and math. Unlike the current educational atmosphere where mathematics instruction is an area of focus, at the time I began teaching, most research and professional development was centered on language arts instruction. Similar to the "math wars" of today, educators heatedly debated the effectiveness of "whole language" instruction as opposed to skills-based instruction. Eventually, a system of "balanced" literacy instruction evolved. While controversy is not always pleasant, it does create a stimulating atmosphere that motivates teachers to reflect on their own experiences in the classroom. My teaching career began in just such an atmosphere, and I benefited from it, eagerly consulting the available research and teaching resources so I could bring the most effective instructional strategies to my classroom.

In the early 2000s, my school system adopted guided reading as part of its balanced literacy initiative. This approach made sense to me. I worked with small groups of students using texts on their instructional levels. The small group approach allowed me to closely monitor the progress of each student and adjust instruction to meet student needs. The success of this instructional method led me to begin using it for mathematics instruction as well. From these experiences in the classroom evolved my first book, *Guided Math: A Framework for Mathematics Instruction* (Sammons 2009).

During my training for guided reading, I was introduced to the book *Mosaic of Thought: Teaching Comprehension in a Reader's Workshop* (1997), authored by Ellin Oliver Keene and Susan Zimmerman. This book asked how teachers could help students become thoughtful, independent readers capable of constructing meaning from what they read. Reading comprehension research identified the strategies most commonly used by proficient readers. By explicitly teaching these comprehension strategies to students, first by modeling and then by releasing responsibility so students could practice on their own, Keene and Zimmerman proposed that students' reading proficiency would improve. Later research confirmed the efficacy of this method. These instructional strategies also made sense to me, and explicitly teaching the reading comprehension strategies espoused in *Mosaic of Thought* became a part of my literacy instruction—with positive results.

As I incorporated balanced literacy and the explicit teaching of comprehension strategies into my language arts curriculum, many similarities between literacy and mathematics instruction became apparent. In both subject areas, students worked, and sometimes struggled, to construct meaning. In reading, they constructed meaning from the words they read. In mathematics, students strived to construct the meaning of mathematical concepts. Moreover, students constructed the meaning of the problems they were asked to solve. Clearly the commonality for success in both subjects was the need for students to construct meaning.

Once that fact dawned on me, I recognized the disconnect between my literacy instruction and my mathematics instruction. Although the goal in each subject area was the same—to help students grow more proficient at constructing meaning—my instructional techniques differed. Even when I employed similar strategies, the terminology differed. I began to think the instructional strategies I used for literacy could also be effective for mathematics comprehension. I began to think that other aspects of literacy instruction would transfer to mathematics—such as the emphasis on building vocabulary knowledge and the use of literature to teach mathematical concepts. Good teaching is good teaching, no matter what the subject. As I reflected on exactly what constitutes "good teaching," many characteristics came to mind. Primary to learning in any subject area is cognition—knowing, perceiving, reasoning. I felt the same teaching strategies I used to prompt students to know, perceive, and reason in reading could also be successfully applied to mathematics with the same result. So, in addition to adapting the guided reading instruction framework to mathematics instruction, I began to borrow and adapt literacy comprehension strategies to use in mathematics.

As might be expected, when I integrated literacy instruction techniques into my mathematics instruction, the alignment between these strategies and the National Council of Teachers of Mathematics (NCTM 2000) process standards became evident. The NCTM process standards require students to communicate, to reason, to make connections, to create multiple representations, and to solve problems—all of which dovetail well with the comprehension strategies.

With the adoption of the Common Core State Standards (CCSS) by many states, this curricular alignment continues. The CCSS's eight Standards for Mathematical Practice include making sense of problems, reasoning abstractly, constructing arguments and critiquing the reasoning of others, constructing mathematical models, using appropriate tools, attending to precision, making use of structure, and looking for and expressing regularity in repeated reasoning. To develop deep conceptual understanding, each of these standards requires that students use the same comprehension strategies taught in reading. I was surprised that more teachers had not made this connection.

When I moved out of the classroom to work with teachers as a coach, I saw some teachers who had begun to weave "literacy" strategies into their math lessons—sometimes using the same terminology, sometimes employing different terminology. Teachers in the Yahoo Guided Math group started to share how they had adapted literacy instructional methods for mathematics. With a great deal of enthusiasm, I began gathering ideas for this book.

It is interesting that much of the current reflection on mathematics instruction is spurred by the current "math wars"—so similar to the "whole language versus basic skills" conflict of years ago. In both subject areas, teachers continue to search for the instructional methods that best serve their students. With the Final Report of the National Mathematics Advisory Panel emphasizing the need for students to develop both procedural proficiency and a deep conceptual understanding of mathematics, I see an emerging "balanced" approach to mathematics instruction.

Teachers who teach both reading and math have an advantage because they have developed a toolbox of instructional strategies that are as appropriate for mathematics understanding as they are for literacy. With this book, I hope to provide teachers, whether they teach reading or not, the tools they need to enhance their mathematics instruction through the use of research-based literacy strategies.

Chapter 1 presents an overview of the links between reading and mathematics. Included is an introduction to the comprehension strategies, the research documenting their effectiveness, and an examination of appropriate teaching methods. **Chapter 2** focuses on the importance of teaching mathematical vocabulary and shows how the instructional techniques used to teach reading can be effectively used to teach mathematics.

Chapters 3 through 9 each highlight one comprehension strategy, providing specific, practical guidance on its application to mathematics instruction. Finally, **Chapter 10** describes how these strategies relate to the Guided Math framework.

The ideas presented in this book provide all teachers with an instructional road map for applying literacy strategies to mathematics instruction. Good teaching is indeed good teaching!

Unfortunately, many students continue to struggle with content area comprehension, failing to recognize that the strategies they learned to help them with their reading comprehension can also be applied to increase their understanding in other subject areas.

Though most educators recognize that reading ability is crucial to success in any subject area, including mathematics, the instructional strategies taught are most commonly partitioned by subject area. Sometimes this occurs because teachers specialize in only one or two subjects. More often, in elementary schools, homeroom teachers use very different strategies when teaching multiple subjects. The lack of consistency in instruction is puzzling. Instructional strategies that teachers use so successfully in reading are often abandoned when they teach mathematics and other content areas. Even when employing similar strategies, the terminology differs. So, even if students are expected to use similar approaches to understanding mathematics, the lack of consistent vocabulary creates confusion and limits the effectiveness of these approaches. As a consequence, student comprehension and understanding suffer.

Reading and Mathematics Connections

In *Comprehending Math: Adapting Reading Strategies to Teach Mathematics K–6*, Hyde (2006) describes how thinking, language, and mathematics are braided together into a "tightly knit entity like a rope that is stronger than the individual strands." Reading is closely linked to thinking and language, and so is mathematics. The three components are inseparable, mutually supportive, and necessary. In reading, students use decoding skills, and then go a step further to construct meaning by interacting with the text. In mathematics, students need to be encouraged to use the same strategies as they construct mathematical meaning (Sammons 2009). In fact, many of the characteristics of good readers are found in good mathematicians (Minton 2007). See figure 1.1 for a side-by-side comparison.

Fig. 1.1. Similarities Between Good Readers and Good Mathematicians

Characteristics of Good Readers	Characteristics of Good Mathematicians
They call upon their prior knowledge to make meaning from text.	They call upon prior knowledge to understand concepts and solve problems.
They are fluent readers.	They are procedurally fluent.
They have a mental image of what they are reading.	They create multiple representations of mathematics concepts and problems.
They use multiple strategies to understand and interpret text.	They use multiple strategies to understand concepts and solve problems.
They monitor their understanding as they read.	They monitor their understanding as they solve problems.
They can clearly explain their interpretation of the text to others.	They can clearly explain their mathematical thinking to others.

(Adapted from Minton 2007)

Because of these similarities between reading and mathematics, it is only logical that strategies employed to increase comprehension in one would be equally as effective at increasing comprehension in the other. Just as teachers are adapting the Guided Reading instructional framework to create the Guided Math framework (Sammons 2009), many teachers are now adapting literacy strategies for mathematics instruction. As Ellin Keene asked in the foreword to Hyde's *Comprehending Math*, "…if we ask kids to construct meaning in reading, wouldn't we ask them to do the same in math?" (Hyde 2006).

Reading and Mathematics Comprehension

Reading in its truest sense requires comprehension, construction of meaning from the written language. In this sense, reading comprehension goes beyond simply decoding words or reading fluently. It is the dynamic process of taking information from the written text, interacting with it, and then using it in a way that demonstrates the reader understands the information. In fact, it may accurately be said that reading is thinking (Hyde 2006).

Good readers are capable of acting on, responding to, or transforming the information that is presented in written text. They are able to go beyond a simple literal recall or retelling. According to the transformational model of reading comprehension, the reader uses his or her own thought processes and prior knowledge, along with the information from the text, to transform it in some way (Brassell and Rasinski 2008), thereby creating meaning.

Just as good readers create meaning for understanding, mathematicians create meaning as they process mathematical concepts and solve problems. Understanding the relationship between the two disciplines can provide teachers with valuable insights to help students more successfully understand the mathematics they encounter in school and in the real world.

Skillful reading requires readers to be active, as does understanding mathematical ideas. Good readers are actively constructing meaning—using what they know about the content of the text within the given context. They use their knowledge of text structure and word meaning as they draw inferences from the words they read (Hyde 2006; Owocki 2003). The same is true for mathematics—in fact, doubly so. Mathematics requires not only the construction of meaning related to mathematical concepts, but also comprehension of the written text that is so often required for problem-solving tasks.

What kinds of knowledge do readers draw upon as they read? According to Owocki (2003), this knowledge includes:

- knowledge about text content
- knowledge about text structure
- pragmatic knowledge
- knowledge about the social/situational context

Knowledge About Content

Readers who are familiar with the general subject of the text they are reading are much more likely to be able to construct meaning from that text. Familiarity with the content provides a foundation for both understanding and for building new knowledge. Hence, children with little background knowledge to build upon often struggle with comprehension. Even for those who have excellent decoding skills and read fluently, meaning eludes them. Consequently, these students frequently become frustrated. What joy is there in trying to "read" something that is incomprehensible? Anyone who has tried to read a technical text about an unfamiliar subject can empathize with the lack of motivation to read that is too often evident in these students.

When students are introduced to new mathematical concepts, the same premise holds true. Students who have some foundation to build upon can make connections and create an understanding of the concept more readily than students who lack the background knowledge. Just as good readers apply existing knowledge or schema to new information, mathematicians must apply their existing knowledge to mathematical concepts or problems to construct meaning (Minton 2007). Teachers can help students in these efforts by providing opportunities for them to build background knowledge to serve as a foundation for the new concept.

Even students who have ample background knowledge can benefit from thinking about and discussing foundational content prior to their reading or math work. Previewing spurs students to begin tapping their reservoir of prior knowledge, so that it's easier to construct meaning from the words they are decoding or the math concepts they are solving.

Knowledge About Structure

Accomplished readers are knowledgeable about the structures of the texts they read and use that knowledge to build meaning. The structure of narrative texts differs considerably from that of nonfiction texts. Immersed in a narrative, a reader expects to be introduced to characters, to identify the setting, and to discover the plot as it unfolds.

When studying a nonfiction text, on the other hand, a reader expects to encounter an organizational structure that helps him or her make sense of the content. A biography may be organized in chronological order. Readers come to expect the story of someone's life to unfold in a logical sequence of events. News stories usually begin with the most important points and then move on to the details. In recipes, the ingredients are listed first, followed by step-by-step directions.

Similarly, the study of mathematics is based on structures. Students benefit from knowing about the structure of word problems—considered by some to be a unique genre. Word problems most often have the introductory information first, then any factual information needed, followed by the main idea—what students need to determine—at the end of the problem. In addition, the discipline itself is replete with structures and frameworks on which mathematical concepts are constructed. For instance, one of the first mathematical structures students learn is that of place value. It is difficult for young learners to understand the concepts of addition or subtraction with regrouping if they do not comprehend place value.

An awareness of both textual and mathematical structures provides scaffolding for students when reading or working with mathematics. When students become aware of both the textual structures of literary genres and the mathematical structures they encounter, they have at their disposal a toolbox of resources for constructing meaning.

Pragmatic Knowledge

In addition to the content knowledge readers use to construct meaning, they also bring a wealth of socio-cultural, or *pragmatic,* knowledge gleaned through years of interactions with others. When filtered through these diverse perspectives, the constructed meanings of texts can vary dramatically. In the same way, students bring their own understandings and experiences into play as they construct mathematical meaning. Many young people have acquired problem-solving strategies outside of school. They call upon these earlier experiences as they tackle mathematical tasks within the classroom. Teachers who allow students a degree of latitude as they solve problems will be rewarded with insight into the pragmatic knowledge of their students. By respecting students' unique attempts at problem solving, teachers increase students' confidence and their willingness to take risks. As students share their strategies, the strategic resources of the entire class are broadened.

When students become aware that their interpretations of a text or strategies for solving problems vary because of the unique pragmatic knowledge that each of them brings to the task, they become aware of the limits of their perspectives, even as their perspectives are expanded.

Knowledge About the Social/Situational Context

Finally, readers are influenced by the situations in which their reading occurs. Reading a poem for the beauty of its language is quite different from reading it when assigned to analyze its meaning. The purpose or goals for reading set by a teacher in a reading assignment can shade the meaning-making of students. Likewise, students reading a mathematics word problem in search of key words may construct a very different interpretation of the problem than students attempting to visualize the problem based on their past experiences and the mathematical connections they recognize.

How teachers frame their expectations and goals for students, whether in reading or mathematics, has an enormous impact on the meanings constructed by their students. Teachers should always be aware of how the goals they set for their students influence how students interpret text or mathematical tasks.

The individual goals and beliefs students have instilled in them both at home and in school are also closely related to their mathematics performance. When students believe that their efforts determine their achievement rather than just their innate ability, they are more persistent in their mathematics learning and, thus, are more successful. The National Research Council (2001) in its study *Adding It Up: Helping Children Learn Mathematics*, referred to a positive attitude toward mathematics as productive disposition. Productive disposition is "the tendency to see sense in mathematics, to perceive it as both useful and worthwhile, to believe that steady effort in learning mathematics pays off, and to see oneself as an effective learner and doer of mathematics." Because of its importance, it is identified as one of the five strands of mathematical proficiency.

Explicit Instruction

Most of us have had experiences in which we suddenly become aware of something that we had never before noticed, but that was right there in front of us. Until it was brought to our attention, we were completely unaware that it existed. Once it became obvious to us, however, it was hard to believe that we could ever have been unaware of it. After all, it was right there.

Remembering experiences like that help us understand the need to explicitly teach our students the comprehension strategies that we use regularly for reading and for mathematical thinking. Since these strategies are used by experienced readers and mathematicians with such ease, there is a tendency to expect them to be obvious to our students. Because they are not necessarily obvious, teaching the strategies explicitly opens the curtains for students, bringing this kind of thinking to their attention and providing valuable tools to enhance their learning.

What is meant by explicit teaching of these strategies? It is not an easy task "to make visible the unseen processes of creating meaning from text" (Murphy 2010). To do it well is one of the greatest challenges teachers face.

Explicit instruction can be broken down into six specific steps (Taylor et al. 1994):

1. Teacher explains *what* the strategy is.

2. Teacher explains *why* the strategy is important.

3. Teacher explains *when* to use the strategy.

4. Teacher *models how* to perform the strategy in an actual context while students observe.

5. Teacher *guides students* as they practice using the strategy.

6. Students *independently* use the strategy.

The emphasis is on *explicit* instruction because too often students are given a strategy (step 1) and are then expected to be able to use it independently (step 6). Without teaching the intermediate steps, students are unlikely to use the strategy. Teachers increase the success of their students when they provide clear explanations of not only the *what*, but also the *why*, *when*, and *how* followed by guided student practice and then finally independent student practice, gradually releasing responsibility to the students (Pearson and Gallagher 1983; Miller 2002). By following each of the six steps, teachers support their students throughout the learning process. Gradually, they withdraw support so students can successfully apply the strategies independently.

Explaining the "What"

Thought should be given to how to introduce a strategy. Before trying to explain a strategy to students, teachers should have a deep understanding of the strategy and how it is used effectively. Careful consideration should be given to the language used to define it. Is the explanation clearly worded and does the definition accurately convey what students need to know? Consistency in vocabulary usage is another consideration since establishing a common classroom language that can be applied across the curriculum is important. Furthermore, explanations should be concise—precisely expressing what the strategy is as well as what it is not.

Explaining the "Why"

The introduction of a strategy most often includes a description, but teachers frequently fail to explain why it is used. While the "why" may seem quite obvious, especially to experienced readers, teachers should be wary of assuming that it is obvious to students. A brief, explicit explanation about why using a specific strategy increases understanding ensures that all students are attuned to its utility.

Explaining "When"

Since it is often assumed that students know why a strategy is used, teachers may also assume that students know when to use it. Unless explicitly stated, students may mistakenly attempt to apply strategies information in texts or math tasks. What is the main idea? What are the most important facts? What is the problem asking? Are there any parts that are irrelevant?

As they work, students *synthesize* the information and extend the meaning of the mathematics text or concept. What conjectures can be made from the patterns observed? How can this be applied to real-life situations? They also look critically at the text or the mathematics as they analyze and evaluate its validity. How well-founded is their reasoning? Are the collections of data reliable? Are there any built-in biases in the mathematical materials?

And, with any mathematical work, it is imperative that students actively *monitor meaning*. Does the reading or solution make sense? If not, what can I do to make sense of it? Do I need to reread? Have I gone back over my work to check for accuracy? Can I explain my understanding?

"After" Strategies

The value of applying comprehension strategies does not end when the initial mathematical reading or work is complete. Good thinking requires reflection. Intentional use of comprehension strategies supports and strengthens the process of reflection. Application of these strategies may be even more effective when students work together to share their thoughts. The strategies listed below are especially appropriate as students look back and reflect.

Students may *make* further *connections* after reading or working with a math concept. How does this relate to other ideas or concepts? What experiences have I had that connect to what I just learned?

Sometimes, during the process of reading about mathematical concepts or problems to be solved, the overall picture is obscured by the details. Students should be encouraged to think back to *determine importance*. What was the most important part of what I read? What are the key aspects of the math concept? Why was solving the math problem a worthwhile task?

Having completed some reading or work with a math problem, it is an excellent time to *synthesize information*. How does everything fit together? What new ideas occurred to me using the information I learned? What conclusions did I reach? Did this change my thinking? How can I apply this to real-life situations? Is there anything that makes me question the validity of this information?

As students reflect, they should continue to *monitor meaning*. Did the reading or the concept make sense? Was the answer reasonable? Do I need to revisit my work to clarify my thinking?

Comprehension Strategies for Conceptual Understanding

When introducing a mathematical concept or problem that makes use of comprehension strategies, consider the four C's: Conception, Connection, Construction, and Comprehension.

- **Conception:** Think about the concept or problem to be introduced. What are the foundations on which it builds? Where will students likely have difficulty? What vocabulary should be introduced? Which comprehension strategy will be most effective to help students develop a deep conceptual understanding?

- **Connection:** Consider the prior knowledge of students. How does the new concept or problem connect with their previous mathematical experiences? How might it connect with experiences they have had outside of school? How might it connect with their interests? When planning how to teach the concept, build upon these connections.

- **Construction:** Allow students to construct the meaning of the concept or problem by introducing important vocabulary, making explicit connections to students' prior experiences, providing hands-on learning opportunities, involving students in problem-solving situations, and encouraging conversations about the math they are learning. Model the use of the comprehension strategies and guide students as they apply them. Use both the "before" and "during" comprehension strategies.

- **Comprehension:** Continuously assess students' comprehension of the concept or problem and adjust instruction to respond to student needs. After mastery, include a reflection activity. This may be conducted with the whole class, in small groups, or in one-on-one conferences, although it tends to be most effective when students are able to share their thoughts with their peers. The ideas of one student often spur further thinking by other students. Ask students to record their thinking in math journals. During this period, have students use the "after" comprehension strategies.

Teaching Comprehension Strategies for Mathematics

Keene and Zimmerman's gradual release planning template for teaching reading comprehension strategies (2007) is easily adapted to mathematics. The template includes four phases: *planning phase, early phase, middle phase,* and *late phase.*

Planning Phase

- Identify the strategy to teach and explore its use in a mathematics context with grade-level colleagues.

- Plan mathematics experiences for students who are conducive to teacher modeling and think-alouds and who may be supported by the use of the identified strategy.

- Share with parents how the strategy relates to mathematics and encourage parents to discuss the strategy at home.

Early Phase

Instructional Focus:

- Think aloud about how mathematicians use the strategy.

- Discuss how they use the strategy when working with mathematical concepts and problems.

- Share how the strategy helps build understanding and aids in problem-solving.

- Model use of the strategy in diverse mathematical contexts.

- Model how to communicate mathematical thinking, both orally and in writing.

- Guide a Math Huddle—student mathematical discussion—

where students work together to apply the strategy; record the process on anchor charts for reference.

- In small groups and conferences, encourage students to articulate their thinking and use of the strategy.

Student Focus:

- Students experiment with the strategy individually, in groups, or as part of a Math Huddle.

- Students share their mathematical thinking through sticky notes, diagrams, math journals, and/or conversations.

Middle Phase

Instructional Focus:

- Think aloud and describe the use of the strategy with increasing complexity.

- Show how to apply the strategy in various contexts.

- Model and think aloud to show how the use of the strategy helps them understand more deeply and permanently.

- Share your mathematical thinking using mathematical vocabulary (orally, in writing, and in diagrams).

- Discuss ways in which the strategy relates to previously studied strategies.

- Confer with students to identify further teaching points and (informally) assess their abilities to use the strategy effectively.

- Create and meet with homogenous groups to provide instruction about using the strategy based on student needs.

- Keep parents informed of student progress.

Student Focus:

- Students apply the strategy in diverse mathematical contexts.

- Students express their mathematical strategic thinking in words (orally and in writing) and in diagrams.

- Students apply the strategy in progressively more difficult mathematical contexts.

- Students show evidence of applying the strategy independently.

- Students explain how they use the strategy and how it improves their understanding.

- Students share their use of the strategy with others to further comprehension.

Late Phase

Instructional Focus:

- Model and think aloud using the strategy in challenging contexts with small homogenous groups (needs-based).

- Demonstrate using the strategy to solve problems or to understand mathematical concepts in unfamiliar contexts.

- Share ways in which the strategy integrates with strategies previously learned.

- Begin the planning phase for the next strategy.

Student Focus:

- Students explain their use of the strategy clearly in conferences and to other students.

- Students apply the strategy and can accurately record their thinking in words (orally and in writing) and in diagrams.

- Students share how they use the strategy independently without prompting from the teacher.

- Students use the strategy in more challenging contexts.

- Students use the strategy flexibly.

- Students appropriately "mix and match" an effective use of strategies according to mathematical contexts.

Chapter Snapshot

Both reading and mathematics require purposeful thinking for the construction of meaning. They both involve teasing out big ideas from a set of discrete words, symbols, or procedures. Readers and mathematicians must be able to generate ideas, to express ideas clearly and with precision, and to justify their thinking to others (Carpenter, Franke, and Levi 2003). Naturally, the same comprehension strategies are effective when applied in either of the disciplines.

These strategies are, however, only a tool for facilitating and extending comprehension—the objective is to improve mathematical comprehension. Unfortunately, when comprehension strategies are taught in some classrooms, students are required to spend large amounts of time learning and practicing the strategies without really knowing the "how to" of applying them to increase understanding. The focus of instruction is the strategies themselves rather than building understanding. This misguided focus not only fails to help students increase their understanding, but also makes reading or mathematics work such a ponderous task that it becomes something students try to avoid.

The four planning phases outlined in this chapter offer guidance on how to teach the comprehension strategies, from modeling and think-alouds, through the gradual release of responsibility to students. With instruction and practice, students learn to choose and then effectively apply strategies that increase their mathematical understanding. Both proficient readers and mathematicians routinely use a combination of strategies in a seamless process that is mainly unconscious (Routman 2003). Instilling that same capacity in students is the ultimate goal in comprehension strategies instruction.

How can teachers provide solid support for the mathematical learning of students whose vocabulary development is minimal? Vocabulary development has long been a focus of literacy instruction. Only recently has mathematics instruction begun to support its development.

One of the most effective ways for students to increase vocabulary is through wide reading (exposure to a variety of texts in different formats). Research shows correlations between a child's vocabulary and the amount the child reads. This method has its drawbacks. Students often have difficulty inferring the meaning of unfamiliar words, particularly with mathematical reading. In addition, the mathematics-specific words students must acquire occur too infrequently to give students the repeated exposure needed to acquire an understanding of their meaning (Marzano and Pickering 2005). Relying on wide reading for vocabulary development only increases the inequities in vocabulary knowledge among students (Beck et al. 2002).

Consequently, there is a need for direct vocabulary instruction. In spite of the fact that most of the words in one's vocabulary are acquired incidentally, for students whose vocabularies are limited, and especially for developing an understanding of the mathematics-specific words that students are unlikely to encounter outside of school, this focused vocabulary instruction is essential for mathematical success.

Direct Vocabulary Instruction

What kind of instruction is most effective in helping students increase their level of vocabulary understanding? Beck et al. (2002) call for robust instruction that is vigorous, strong, and powerful in effect. They contend that the meanings of words should be clearly explained and follow-up instruction should provide opportunities for students to engage in thought-provoking, playful, and interactive activities in which the new vocabulary is revisited.

Marzano (2004) presents eight research-based characteristics of effective direct vocabulary instruction:

1. Effective vocabulary instruction does not rely on definitions.

Traditional vocabulary instruction has always focused on dictionary or glossary definitions. Students looked up and then copied the definitions of newly introduced words. This approach has proved to be ineffective, sometimes counterproductive. Students with limited vocabulary development often find that the definitions for new vocabulary words contain words that are also unknown, and the reading level of the definition itself is too difficult, creating frustration and causing students to lose sight of the goal. Students just go "through the motions": they locate the words and copy the definitions with no thought to meaning. This approach undermines attempts to increase student interest in learning new words. In addition, since many definitions tend to be vague with little guidance as to context, students often misinterpret the definitions. Instead of clarifying meaning, the result is an even greater misunderstanding. In no sense can this method of teaching vocabulary be considered robust.

2. Students must represent their knowledge of words in linguistic and nonlinguistic ways.

Since mathematics communication relies on symbols as much as on words, this characteristic also applies to the knowledge of symbols. Dual coding theory of cognition suggests that all knowledge is dependent upon representation and processing by both a verbal or linguistic mode and a nonverbal or nonlinguistic mode (Sadowski 2005). Therefore, for information to be anchored in permanent memory, it must have both linguistic (language-based) and non-linguistic (imagery-based) representations (Marzano 2004). Students' knowledge is deepened when they interact with a new term in both verbal and nonverbal ways. Nonverbal interaction includes creating graphic representations, composing mental images, or acting out the meaning of the terms.

3. Effective vocabulary instruction involves the gradual shaping of word meanings through multiple exposures.

Levels of word knowledge vary greatly and deepen over time according to Beck et al (2002), as shown in figure 2.2.

Fig. 2.2. A Continuum of Word Knowledge

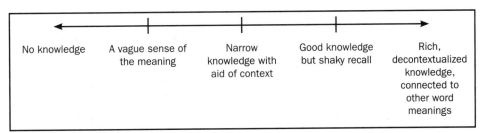

| No knowledge | A vague sense of the meaning | Narrow knowledge with aid of context | Good knowledge but shaky recall | Rich, decontextualized knowledge, connected to other word meanings |

(Adapted from Beck et al. 2002)

Just as the size of a snowball expands as it is rolled along the ground to create a snowman, word knowledge increases and becomes more refined with each additional exposure to a word or symbol. Effective vocabulary instruction includes multiple opportunities for students to revisit terms to deepen and extend their understanding.

4. Students should learn word parts to enhance understanding of terms.

The knowledge of roots and affixes may allow students to determine the meaning of unfamiliar words or to recall the meanings of words that they have forgotten. For example, knowledge of the meaning of *centi-* or *milli-* can give students valuable clues as to the meaning of words containing those parts.

5. Different words require different types of instruction.

The types of words encountered during literacy instruction differ from those that students come across during mathematics, which are much more content-specific. The types of words taught during mathematics instruction frequently relate to properties, relationships, quantities, shapes, measurements, and operations. Whenever possible, these are terms that should be taught in context and through the use of concrete, hands-on methods.

6. Students should discuss the terms they are learning.

When students are engaged in using the new words they learn in context, they gain a deeper understanding of the words, and it increases the likelihood that they will be stored in their permanent memory for later use (Marzano 2004). By using the newly-learned words orally, students move from having a receptive understanding to developing a productive understanding. Planned opportunities for classroom mathematical discourse related to mathematics concepts or problem solving allow students to practice using new vocabulary in authentic contexts.

7. Students should play with words.

Teachers typically include the use of math games to reinforce understanding of math concepts and to promote fact fluency, but less frequently to develop facility with new vocabulary. Games provide additional exposure to the vocabulary words and symbols learned through enjoyable and meaningful experiences. These experiences can inspire a curiosity about words that leads to greater vocabulary acquisition by students because of their increased interest in words in general.

8. **Instruction should focus on terms that have a high probability of enhancing academic success.**

   This characteristic should come as no surprise to teachers. With the limited instructional time available, it is imperative that the terms be those that lead students to a greater mathematical proficiency.

Based on these eight characteristics, Marzano and Pickering (2005) espouse this six-step process for teaching new words.

Step 1: Provide a description, explanation, or example of the new term. (This should not be a dictionary definition. Instead, it should be in words that are readily understood by students.)

Step 2: Ask students to restate the description, explanation, or example in their own words.

Step 3: Ask students to construct a picture, symbol, or graphic representing the term or phrase.

Step 4: Engage students periodically in activities that help them add to their knowledge of the terms in vocabulary notebooks.

Step 5: Periodically ask students to discuss the terms with one another.

Step 6: Involve students in games that allow them to play with terms.

The first three steps are completed within a relatively short period of instructional time. The emphasis during this phase is on explaining the meaning of the vocabulary word in a way that can be understood by students. Unless there is at least an initial understanding of the meaning, the remaining steps are of little use. Teachers may need to relate the word's meaning to students' prior knowledge or to something relevant and of interest to them. It may help to show a concrete example of the term or a video clip for visual reinforcement of the meaning.

Having students restate a word's meaning in their own words allows teachers to check the accuracy of the students' understanding and encourages students to make the word their own. Furthermore, by having students create nonlinguistic representations of the meaning of the words, students demonstrate again the accuracy of their understanding, but also engage in self-created mental imagery thereby increasing the degree and quality of their word learning (Sadowski 2005).

These first three steps of the process are often observed in classrooms, particularly where reading vocabulary is the target. The final three steps, although equally as important to vocabulary learning, are not implemented as consistently. Those steps involve students revisiting the words in ways that are highly motivating for students. Repeated exposure to the new vocabulary is essential. Since word knowledge is a continuum—moving from an initial vague sense of the meaning of a word to a rich, fully developed understanding—it is only through repeated exposures to words in a variety of contexts and formats that functional word knowledge is attained.

With the fourth step, teachers may ask students to review their definitions and graphic representations of the terms, revise them if they wish, and then self-assess their current understanding of the terms. Graphic organizers may be generated by students in which they explore the relationships between mathematically-related words and symbols. The fifth step requires students to use the words in discussions with others. This oral practice increases the level of vocabulary knowledge by moving it from *receptive* vocabulary, where students are capable of understanding these words when listening or reading, to *productive* vocabulary, where students are able to use the words appropriately and in context when speaking or writing (Lehr, Osborn, and Hiebert 2004). Finally, the last step has students participate in games to play with the recently learned vocabulary terms.

The last three steps help students to continue to build meaning for the vocabulary terms as they return to these terms repeatedly and in varying contexts. The repetition helps fuse the words and their meaning into students' receptive and productive vocabularies (Bruner 2001). Since few students encounter this language outside of school, providing opportunities to interact with recently learned words is especially important when teaching mathematics vocabulary. While the Building Academic Vocabulary process is a sound one, there is an essential component of vocabulary instruction that it does not address. As students learn mathematics, one concept often builds on another. In these situations, the meanings of much of the mathematical vocabulary depend on the understanding of previously studied concepts. As a prerequisite for comprehending the new terms, students must have learned and retained an understanding of the foundational concepts on which the new terms rest. This is particularly true in content-specific vocabulary.

To effectively teach mathematical vocabulary, teachers should consider what foundational conceptual knowledge is a prerequisite for understanding the terms and then informally assess their students to assure that they possess the necessary prior knowledge. If the assessments show that students lack the prerequisite knowledge, teachers may have to review or even re-teach concepts that were assumed to have been mastered, and, if necessary, provide concrete or symbolic models of the foundational concepts. When the new terms are introduced, they should be explicitly linked to that foundational prior knowledge, thus leading students to make connections on which they can more readily construct new meaning.

Mathematical texts traditionally introduce new vocabulary at the very beginning of a unit or lesson. Teachers may consider waiting to introduce new terms until after the relevant idea or concept has been explored. It makes more sense cognitively to plan lessons that let students develop an understanding of the concept before the word for that concept is taught. In other words, "allow language to follow concept development" (Thompson et al. 2008).

Choosing Mathematics Terms to Teach

According to Duffy (2003), vocabulary words are of two kinds. There are *content* words that describe concepts for which we have mental pictures. These include things that we have experienced such as happy, run, dogs, or television. There are also *function* words that signal grammatical functions. Such words include *the*, *and*, *is*, and *to*. Although these are used throughout our communications, we do not form mental pictures of them. The content words are the focus of vocabulary instruction—although some students may need support as they encounter *function* words in a mathematical context.

Stahl and Nagy (2005) recommend three types of words to teach students:

1. **Words that are already in students' oral vocabularies, which they need to recognize in print**

   In mathematics, these are the words that students are likely to encounter in solving word problems. For primary students, these might be words such as *how*, *many*, and *more*. Upper elementary students who experience difficulties with decoding words may struggle while solving problems that include words such as *pitcher*, *favorite*, *practiced*, and *receive* even though they most likely already know the meaning of these words. To be successful mathematically, it is important that students develop the skills to independently decode these words.

   Instructional strategies for teaching decoding skills are not included in this chapter. Instead, the focus is on helping students learn the meanings of unfamiliar words. Nevertheless, one of the most effective strategies students can employ to decode words like these is the use of context clues, including looking closely at any pictures and thinking about what makes sense in the sentence.

2. **Words that are not in students' oral vocabularies, but that are labels for concepts already familiar to students**

   For the purposes of mathematics vocabulary instruction, these words might include *quantity*, *comparison*, *complete*, *connect*, *item*, and *exact*. Young learners usually understand the concepts these words represent, but may not know the more mathematically specific words. These words should be explicitly taught. Teachers should scan grade-level mathematics resources searching for words that may prevent students from understanding a problem in spite of their possessing the mathematical skill needed to solve it. Once these words have been identified, they should be included as part of the vocabulary instruction.

3. Words not in students' oral vocabularies that refer to new concepts

These are the most important words mathematics vocabulary instruction should target. Examples of these words are *parallel*, *isosceles*, *area*, *array*, and *circumference*. Since mathematical terms like these are seldom used or encountered by students outside the school environment, providing effective daily vocabulary support is instrumental in supporting the mathematical achievement of students. With mathematics-specific words, teachers should help students become aware of any multiple meanings for these words. Some mathematical terms have definitions that are very different when they are used in everyday contexts. An awareness of the multiple meanings prior to encountering them in a mathematical context can prevent confusion and misunderstanding by students.

What mathematics terms should teachers introduce explicitly? Ideally, a team of teachers should examine the mathematics standards for their grade level to identify the terms students *must know* to understand the concepts, skills, and processes they are expected to master during the year. Teachers working together to create the list of essential mathematical vocabulary words have the advantage of providing multiple viewpoints and experiences.

If a collaborative process for selecting essential mathematics vocabulary is not possible, a pair of teachers or even an individual teacher can assemble a vocabulary list based on the mathematics curriculum. In some schools, grade-level mathematics vocabulary lists are assembled at a district level. Having teachers directly involved, however, leads to a deep understanding of the terms chosen, a knowledge of why these words were chosen, buy-in to the compiled list, and, as a result, more effective vocabulary instruction.

Mink (2010) provides the following guidelines that teachers may follow for selecting the essential vocabulary:

1. Read the standard or objective correlated to the concepts to be taught.

2. Choose specific content words necessary for student understanding to access the mathematics in that standard or objective.

3. Consider other vocabulary words that students need to grasp in order to have mastery of the standard or objective.

4. Combine the lists to create a master list of vocabulary words for instruction.

A comprehensive list is comprised of terms from the current grade-level standards, significant terms from previous years (so they can be reviewed and reinforced), as well as selected terms that will be introduced in subsequent years, so they may be "previewed" when appropriate. These reviews and previews do not have to be extensive—just ways of reminding students what they have already learned and encouraging them to make connections in anticipation of learning related math concepts.

Some states now provide mathematical vocabulary lists by grade level as part of their standards, thereby making it easier for teachers to be certain that their vocabulary instruction aligns with the state standards. The alignment of standards and instruction is crucial for student success on state-mandated tests where the language of the test is drawn specifically from the standards. The vocabulary of the mathematics standards differs from state to state, as do the definitions of some of these terms. Because of these differences, the mathematical terms used in textbooks may vary significantly from those included in state standards. Accordingly, although mathematics textbooks may be valuable resources, it is imperative that teachers not rely on them as the sole source of the mathematics vocabulary they teach (Riccomini and Witzel 2009). Teachers have the responsibility of ensuring that the mathematics vocabulary they teach their students is well-aligned to their state standards.

Engaging Students in Learning Mathematical Vocabulary

Moving beyond the "look it up and write the definition" mode of mathematical vocabulary instruction may present a challenge for some teachers. The demands of helping students retain mastery of previously taught concepts and skills as they develop a deep understanding of new concepts, while meeting the diverse needs of an entire class of students, in addition to providing effective instruction on mathematical vocabulary, may be daunting. Whew! Just thinking about these many tasks is exhausting. Reflecting on how these demands are interwoven, however, may help teachers come to grips with their myriad of mathematical instructional responsibilities.

The understanding and precise use of mathematical vocabulary by students are critical components of the NCTM process standards (2000) and reinforce the belief that mathematics and language are interconnected (Thompson et al. 2008). As such, teaching vocabulary is relevant across the mathematical domains. Rather than seeing vocabulary instruction as an add-on to what is already occurring during mathematics instruction, it may be viewed as a method of enhancing instructional effectiveness.

The instructional activities described in this chapter may be seamlessly integrated into the everyday instructional practices of teachers: providing activating strategies, buttressing lessons for whole group instruction, complementing small group instruction, presenting engaging tasks for math workshops, supplying teaching points for conferences, and even affording opportunities for formative assessment. As Murray (2004) describes her middle school mathematics instructional approach, "the vocabulary focus of my classroom is not an add-on to the curriculum, or *more* to teach; it is a *way* to teach mathematics. Learning and using mathematics vocabulary becomes a part of the way we do business."

Encouraging Parental Involvement

Enlisting the support of parents is an effective way to promote the use of mathematical vocabulary outside the school environment. Parents play a pivotal role in their child's learning and involving them can maximize the effectiveness of vocabulary instruction. Murray (2004) begins the school year with a letter to parents explaining the vocabulary focus of her classroom and inviting their support. She then follows up with frequent bulletins to keep parents updated. Her communications with parents consistently convey the message that studying mathematics vocabulary is worthwhile and that it increases the mathematics competency of their children. She asks that parents encourage their children to discuss their mathematics vocabulary work at home because "every opportunity to use the language helps students develop a deeper understanding of the mathematics and supports their ability to communicate their mathematical reasoning."

By including parents in the learning process, not only are opportunities for mathematical communication outside the school setting encouraged, but as a consequence of these mathematical discussions with parents, students gain insights into the relevance of mathematics to their lives and those of their family members. Through mathematical conversations with family members, students are better able to connect the mathematical concepts they are studying in school to real-life applications. Parents may also be asked to assist their children in finding mathematics language in locations outside of school and in the media. When an instance is found, students can bring in the example and share it with the class. These activities help students recognize the pervasiveness of mathematics in the world in which they live.

Mathematical Discourse

Just as learning a foreign language is easiest when the learner is thoroughly immersed in the language, the same principle holds true for learning mathematical vocabulary. The benefits of creating a classroom community in which mathematical discourse is the norm are great. If students are to develop competence as mathematical thinkers, they need to have an understanding of mathematical words and symbols. That understanding must extend beyond knowing the "definition" to the ability to use the words with some precision to describe mathematical thoughts, observations, and reasoning. Carefully planned and guided mathematical class conversations help students not only develop the necessary understanding, but give them practice using the terminology (Chapin, O'Connor, and Anderson 2003).

Mathematical conversations may begin with the use of language that is familiar to students. Building on the prior knowledge of their students, the teacher models the use of more precise and meaningful mathematical vocabulary. Students hear the terms used in context and are encouraged to use them during discussions (Murray 2004). In addition to providing opportunities for students to hone their understanding and use of the vocabulary, the focus on the mathematical concepts around which the discussions revolve serves to enhance the conceptual knowledge of students.

Furthermore, these conversations allow students to become true doers of mathematics, interacting with one another as mathematicians do, using meaningful mathematics vocabulary that has a shared meaning. In the course of classroom discussions about relevant mathematics-related problems and issues, the image of mathematics as a discipline is elevated from its stereotype as a dry, straight-from-the-book subject to a living, breathing, intriguing matter for consideration.

For teachers, mathematical discourse by students "provides a lens for accessing and assessing what students understand and how they understand the mathematics they are expected to learn…[it] helps make evident what mathematics content processes our students know as well as how they know it (e.g., procedurally, conceptually, through memorization, or by making connections to real-world problems)" (Thompson et al. 2008). The insights gained by listening to students' own descriptions of their understanding far exceed what is gained from a traditional paper and pencil math test. They allow teachers to refine their instruction to target areas of vocabulary or conceptual misunderstanding and plan the next instructional steps based on the specific needs of their students.

Careful and considered teacher planning leads to successful mathematical discussions among students. When structured around problem solving, the choice of a problem is the key to motivating student talk. Ideally, the problem has no one correct answer or solution method and is relevant to the students. Initial conversation may focus on helping students determine the meaning of the problem, what information is provided, whether any additional information is needed, and what they are asked to find out. During the problem-solving process, students are encouraged to share their observations, describe their thinking about the problem, and share their ideas about possible strategies to use to solve the problem. Once completed, discussion revolves around the solutions and how students went about the process of solving the problem.

The discussion format may vary: whole group, small group, or pairs of students. If the discussion is to be whole group, it is beneficial to ask partners to talk together first, so that students have an opportunity to try out their ideas in a nonthreatening situation before sharing them with the whole group. Once students have shared their thoughts with a partner, they tend to be more comfortable sharing with the whole group. Whatever the format, teachers need to ensure that the overall environment is risk-free. Mistakes should be considered opportunities for learning. All attempts at sharing mathematical ideas should be valued and supported.

Teachers' questions impact the quality of mathematical discussions by students. Questions that support exploring, probing, and sharing inspire student conversation filled with rich, meaningful vocabulary usage. Developing quality questions requires planning. Consider what issues may arise during a conversation and plan questions that lead not to just a "correct" answer, but that encourage students to extend the discussion beyond simple answers.

Murray (2004) suggests the following techniques for composing questions that encourage vocabulary use:

Teachers should provide students with descriptive feedback on their written communication, pointing out what they have done well and providing suggestions for improvement. The teacher commentary is most effective when it includes the language of the standards and lets students know precisely how they need to improve their work so it meets the standard. The ongoing checking of their students' mathematical writing provides teachers with a productive way to monitor their students' understanding so any misconceptions can be corrected.

Mathematics Word Walls

Word walls have become a hallmark of literacy instruction. Posting frequently used words in alphabetical order on a classroom wall or bulletin board creates an ongoing display that students use as a reference while writing and as a basis for word games that strengthen vocabulary skills. For literacy instruction, word walls usually consist of words whose meaning students already know. A word wall allows students to spell the words correctly as they use them in writing.

Mathematics word walls also support students' efforts at spelling mathematical terms correctly. In addition, these word walls scaffold the learning of mathematics vocabulary by including not only a correct spelling of the word or depiction of the symbol, but also a graphic representation of the meaning of the term to aid students as they try to recall its meaning. Students may refer to the word walls as they write, during mathematical discussions to find the specific word they need, or to recall what a math word or symbol means.

A math word wall may also be the basis for mathematical vocabulary games as recommended in the sixth step of Marzano's and Pickering's process for teaching academic vocabulary (Marzano and Pickering 2005). Many games may be created and played using this resource. For example, a teacher may think of a word and challenge students to guess it as clues are given. Students may be asked to find ways to group or sort the words (other than in alphabetical order) and then challenge other students to figure out the criteria for the grouping. The teacher might give the students a topic and ask that they find all the words that are related to it (O'Connell 2007). Ongoing interaction with the words on the word wall enhances students' mathematical vocabulary knowledge.

In creating a mathematics word wall, location is important. Students should be able to see the words from their work areas. Words should be written on strips of tag board in letters large enough to be easily read and include a picture or nonlinguistic representation. Add words to the display as they are introduced so that they are meaningful to students. While words in literacy word walls are grouped alphabetically, consider grouping math words by domain or concept. If space is limited, remove words from the wall when moving to another math topic. However, it is preferable to leave all words displayed once they have been introduced, so students can continue to refer to them. This also provides an easy way to review cumulative vocabulary knowledge and helps dispel the notion that mathematics is a set of unrelated units. Two examples of word walls are shown in figures 2.5 (below) and 2.6 (next page).

Fig. 2.5. Sample Math Word Wall 1

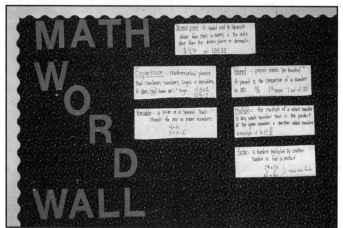

Fig. 2.6. Sample Math Word Wall 2

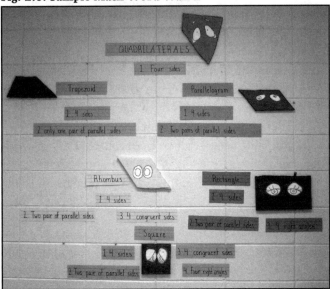

Graphic Organizers

Using graphic organizers is a powerful way for students to refine their understanding of the mathematical vocabulary they are learning. These visual displays show the relationships among ideas. According to Fountas and Pinnell (2001), use of graphic organizers can help students:

- see how ideas are organized or organize their own ideas

- use a concrete representation to understand abstract ideas

- arrange information so it is easier to recall

- understand the hierarchy of ideas (from larger to smaller)

- understand the interrelationship of complex ideas

These tools aid students as they organize their thinking about the new terms and provide a structure for recording these organizational patterns—making the content visual for learners (Thompson and Thomason 2005). Their use helps students retain the meaning of new terms by becoming "blueprints" of the abstract ideas, making them more visible and concrete.

Furthermore, completing graphic organizers requires that students rethink what they have learned about a word or symbol, compelling them to locate information and determine relationships between words and concepts. Graphic organizers depict key thinking skills that promote active thinking about the vocabulary terms. Through the process of organizing their thinking in these formats, students are led to see the terms as components of larger concepts rather than isolated facts (Thompson and Thomason 2005). As with any written work, students need teacher feedback leading them to correct misconceptions, deepen and extend their understanding, and recognize connections to the background knowledge they bring to the task (Mink 2010).

Introduce a graphic organizer with modeling and think-alouds. Choose a mathematics vocabulary term and then share your thinking while completing each section of the graphic organizer. When students are familiar with the format, lead the class or a small group of students in completing the same type of graphic organizer on chart paper, but this time with a different vocabulary term. Simultaneously, students may complete individual graphic organizers in their math journals. Once students are comfortable working with the graphic organizer, ask them to complete one with the same format, but a different vocabulary term, independently or as a group project. Display both chart-size graphic organizers and smaller individual graphic organizers to remind students of the format of the organizer and how it is used.

Many types of graphic organizers have been developed for use in the classroom. The following are a few effective examples:

Frayer Diagram: A modified Frayer diagram (figure 2.7 and Appendix A) may be used to promote vocabulary knowledge. Typically, in a Frayer diagram, the vocabulary word goes in the center. At the top-left corner is the definition of the word; at the top-right are characteristics of the word; at the bottom-left corner are examples of the word; and at the bottom-right are non-examples. In the modified version, students draw a nonlinguistic representation in the upper-right corner.

Fig. 2.7. Sample Frayer Diagram

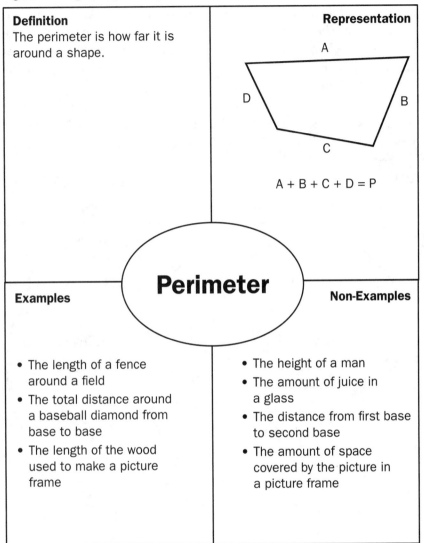

Definition
The perimeter is how far it is around a shape.

Representation

A

D

B

C

$$A + B + C + D = P$$

Perimeter

Examples

- The length of a fence around a field
- The total distance around a baseball diamond from base to base
- The length of the wood used to make a picture frame

Non-Examples

- The height of a man
- The amount of juice in a glass
- The distance from first base to second base
- The amount of space covered by the picture in a picture frame

Venn Diagram: Venn diagrams allow students to graphically display the mathematical relationships of terms or concepts. Loops represent groups that share properties. Most frequently, two overlapping rings are used for comparison (figure 2.8). The shared properties are indicated by the overlapping area. Venn diagrams may also be composed of rings within rings to illustrate sets that are included within other sets. For example, squares have all the characteristics of rectangles; rectangles have all the characteristics of quadrilaterals. To represent their relationships, the Venn diagram has a large ring for the quadrilaterals. Within that ring, is a smaller ring for the rectangles. Within that ring, is an even smaller ring for the squares (figure 2.9).

Fig. 2.8. Venn Diagram Comparing Squares and Rectangles

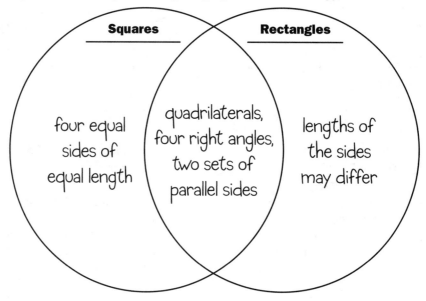

Fig. 2.9. Venn Diagram Showing Relationships Between Quadrilaterals, Rectangles, and Squares

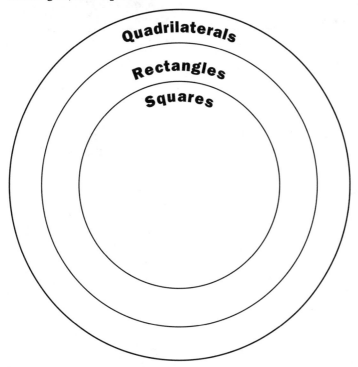

"These Are.../These Are Not..." Chart: These charts provide a relatively simple way to help students distinguish the characteristics that define a concept or symbol. They are particularly useful when used to differentiate between concepts that have properties that are closely related and frequently confused (Thompson et al. 2008). For example, the terms *similar* and *congruent* are often confused by students. Creating a "These Are/These Are Not" chart for *congruent shapes* either as a class, in small groups, in pairs, or individually helps students clearly understand that congruent shapes must be the same size as well as *similar* (figure 2.10). The discussion spurred by the generation of these visual displays reveals to students the similarities and differences between the two terms. Other terms that could be compared using this type of chart are the concepts of *composite* and *not composite,* or *prime,* numbers (figure 2.11).

Fig. 2.10. "These Are.../These Are Not..." Chart for Congruent Shapes

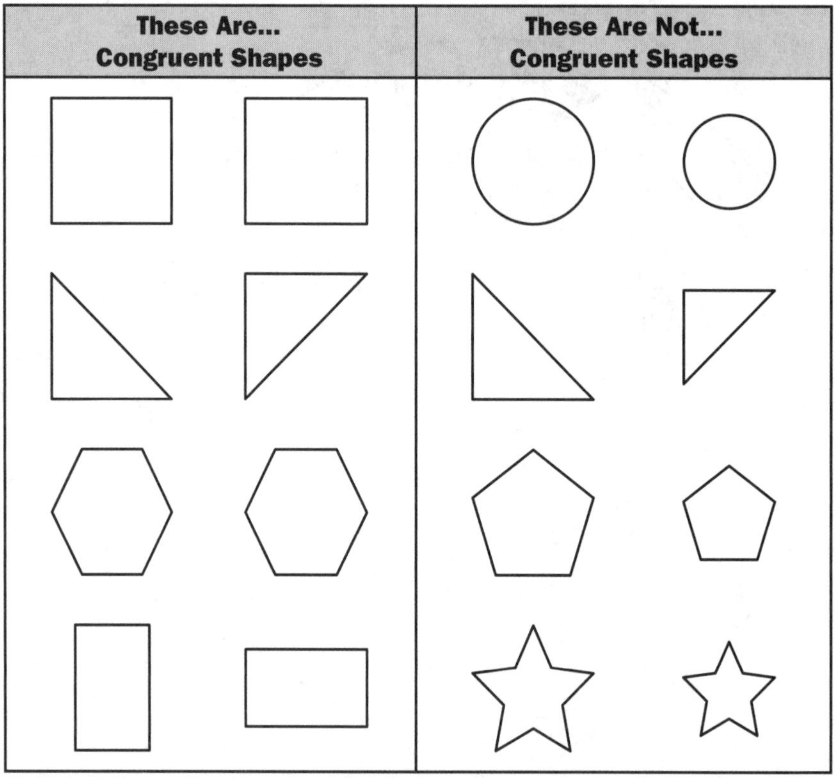

These Are... Congruent Shapes	These Are Not... Congruent Shapes

(Adapted from Thompson et al. 2008)

Fig. 2.11. "These Are.../These Are Not..." Chart for Composite Numbers

These Are... Composite Numbers	These Are Not... Composite Numbers
4	2
100	29
63	$\frac{1}{2}$
1,000,000	1,621
27	401

(Adapted from Thompson et al. 2008)

Matrix or Semantic Features Analysis Grid: These graphic displays provide a format to organize information about ideas or concepts (figure 2.12). In the left-hand column, students list the terms to be compared. In the top row, they list the characteristics or properties.

Once the cells are filled, similarities and differences are evident (Marzano and Pickering 2005; Thompson et al. 2008).

Fig. 2.12. Shape Matrix

(Key: + has the attribute; — does not have the attribute)

Shape	Four Sides	Four Equal Sides	Four Right Angles	Two Pairs of Parallel Sides
Quadrilateral	+	–	–	–
Square	+	+	+	+
Rectangle	+	–	+	+
Rhombus	+	+	–	+
Parallelogram	+	–	–	+
Trapezoid	+	–	–	–

(Adapted from Marzano and Pickering 2005; Thompson et al. 2008)

Concept Map: The development of concept maps leads students to see connections between vocabulary terms and concepts (figure 2.13). Creating the maps links prior knowledge with the study of new vocabulary terms. A specific term is written at the center of the map. Extending from it are the connecting links—lines leading to related terms or concepts. Growing out from the center, the words become more specific. The maps vary in complexity based on students' prior knowledge. When used at the beginning of instruction, they may serve to check prior knowledge. Later, encourage students to add to the original concept maps as they gain an understanding of the terms. Use concept maps as a formative assessment of student vocabulary knowledge (Thompson and Thomason 2005; Thompson et al. 2008; O'Connell 2007).

Fig. 2.13. Sample Concept Map for Multiplication

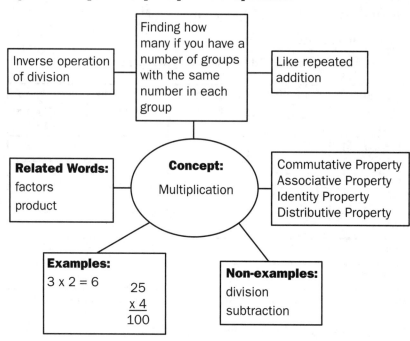

(Adapted from Thompson and Thomason 2005; Thompson et al. 2008; O'Connell 2007)

There are numerous varieties of graphic organizers that students may employ to broaden and extend their understanding of mathematical vocabulary terms. Check websites or other teacher instructional resources for additional ideas. By creating visual displays of the new terms, students are apt to develop a deeper and more complex understanding of their meanings.

Games and Other Learning Activities

Games may be valuable as instructional tools. The sixth step of Marzano's and Pickering's (2005) *Building Academic Vocabulary* supports involving students in games that allow them to play with vocabulary terms. Combining learning with play is highly motivational and contributes to the word consciousness of students. The following are examples of effective games that help increase mathematical vocabulary.

Vocabulary Charades

Similar to the traditional game of charades, participants silently act out an idea or word while others try to guess what they are acting out (Thompson et al. 2008; Marzano and Pickering 2005). The kinesthetic nature of this game helps make mathematical terms concrete for some learners. This may be played in two different ways. Ask students to stand by their desks and show the meaning of a term using their arms, legs, and bodies. In the second, form teams of students. Choose one member of each team to act out a given vocabulary term while others try to guess it as quickly as possible. For example:

- *Parallel lines* might be shown by holding arms parallel to each other.

- The *x-axis* may be shown with arms outstretched horizontally.

- *Circumference* could be illustrated by arms in a circle.

- *Symmetry* can be demonstrated by having the arm and leg on the left side of the body in the same position as the arm and leg on the right side of the body.

This game works well as a closing activity or for a brief break between lessons. It also allows teachers to informally assess the vocabulary knowledge of students so any misconceptions may be addressed.

Make My Day

This game encourages students to listen carefully as they demonstrate their understanding of mathematical terms and concepts. Each student is given a large card on which is written a vocabulary term, figure, number, or an expression. Students listen for clues from the teacher. If the student's card matches the clue, he or she steps forward to "make the teacher's day" (Thompson et al. 2008).

In a primary classroom, use cards with addition and subtraction problems may be used. Call out: "If you have a sum of 10, Make My Day"; "If you have a difference of 4, Make My Day"; "If one of your addends is 2, Make My Day."

In an upper elementary classroom studying factors and multiples, give students cards with clues such as: "If you are a factor of 24, Make My Day"; "If you are a multiple of 3, Make My Day"; "If you are a multiple of both 3 and 2, Make My Day."

In a middle school class, give students number cards and clues such as: "If you have the sum of -5 and 6, Make My Day"; "If you have the product of -5 and 6, Make My Day"; "If you have the quotient of -6 divided by 3, Make My Day."

With this game, not only is vocabulary knowledge reinforced but students' listening skills are also honed. As the game progresses, reteach when necessary and help students refine their understanding of the new vocabulary terms.

I Have, Who Has?

Each student receives a card with two statements: *I have_____. Who has _____?* One student reads his or her card, which has been filled in by the teacher with vocabulary terms or mathematical concepts. The student with the answer to the question stands. This student then reads his or her card, and the game continues (Murray 2004; Mink 2010).

Some examples of how to use appropriate game cards for a variety of grade levels include:

- **First student:** I have *2 + 3.* Who has *7 doubled?*
  Second student: I have *14.* Who has *3^2?*

- **First student:** I have *a pentagon.* Who has *a right angle?*
  Second student: I have *90°.* Who has an *arc?*

- **First student:** I have *congruent sides.* Who has *a number with more than two factors?*

- **Second student:** I have *36.* Who has *180°?*

Like Make My Day, this game sharpens the listening skills of students while strengthening their understanding of new vocabulary terms.

Math Hunt

In a Math Hunt (Mink 2010), teams of students spend a week gathering items that represent the terms they are studying. If students build a model or a collage of the word, they receive four points. A picture of the word earns three points. If they find a book or magazine about the word, they get two points. Finally, they receive one point for drawing a picture of the word or writing a sentence in which the word is used correctly. After some initial planning time, teams are given time to search for items using books, the Internet, magazines, and any other resources available. At the end of the week, students share the items they collected and points are tallied. The winning team creates a classroom display of the vocabulary words with the items collected.

The ongoing nature of this game keeps students focused and encourages them to discover new vocabulary terms in and out of school. Additionally, the collaborative approach leads to authentic math talk within the teams.

Talk a Mile a Minute

Provide a list of related words belonging to a specified category. Each team designates a "talker" who sees the list of words. During the game, the "talker" tries to elicit the correct words from his or her team by describing them as quickly and accurately as possible without using any words in the category title or any rhyming words. The "talker" keeps talking until all the terms have been identified or time has been called (Marzano and Pickering 2005).

The following might be categories and lists of words:

- Kinds of measurement: area, perimeter, volume, temperature, weight, length, time

- Solid shapes: cones, cylinders, cubes, rectangular prisms, pyramids, spheres

- Kinds of numbers: irrational, prime, whole, composite, rational, odd, integers

This game encourages both receptive and productive vocabulary development. The "talker" must thoroughly understand the term and be able to generate ways to describe it, while the rest of the team must be able to produce the word based on the descriptions.

Of course, many games may be played to reinforce new vocabulary. For a comprehensive and lasting knowledge of new terms and concepts, interaction with vocabulary should be ongoing. The process of revisiting and playing with the words and symbols helps students retain the meanings and develop the capacity to use the terms accurately in oral and written mathematical communication.

Literature Links to Mathematical Vocabulary Acquisition

Literature is a natural fit for mathematical vocabulary instruction. People are drawn to the allure of a well-told story, especially if read aloud. Throughout history, lessons have been taught through the language of stories. Long before the era of textbooks, people shared their wisdom through oral communication. Common understandings developed through these storytelling experiences.

In spite of the technology they have at their fingertips, most students are still spellbound when they listen to a good story. Use literature to introduce, reinforce, and review the meaning of mathematical vocabulary words. Mathematically-related books show mathematics in context, so students experience it in ways that seem real to them.

Hearing mathematical terms used in the context of a story or nonfiction text supports students as they develop their mathematical thinking and communication skills in a nonthreatening way (O'Connell 2007). The discussion generated through teacher questioning encourages students to use the vocabulary as they share their own mathematical ideas. In addition, the discussion can provide information that leads to a deeper understanding of the words or concepts.

Using mathematics-related literature when introducing vocabulary for a unit of study can be an effective activating strategy. Not only is it enjoyable, but it also adds to a sense of classroom community as students share in a common experience. Brainstorming about the content prior to the read-aloud activates students' prior knowledge (Thompson et al. 2008). The predictions made during the brainstorming help focus students' attention as the story is read without interruption.

A second reading offers the occasion to pause and highlight mathematical content, vocabulary, and connections. Picture books are particularly valuable in helping students learn new vocabulary. As described earlier in this chapter, having pictures related to the terms promotes student understanding of the new vocabulary. Students enjoy rereading familiar texts, so the stories may be returned to for additional readings.

To further enhance the value of mathematics-related literature, teachers may work with students to create charts of the math terms, their definitions, and how they were used in the literature. These charts may be displayed in the classroom for students to use as a reference when working with this vocabulary.

Chapter Snapshot

An understanding of critical mathematical terms is essential for students as they develop an understanding of mathematical concepts. Whereas reading vocabulary is frequently learned through incidental exposure to the words in everyday conversations and through wide reading, mathematical terms are rarely encountered outside of school. It is imperative that these words and concepts be taught directly to students.

Either on your own or in a grade-level team, compile lists of mathematical vocabulary terms for each grade level through careful examination of the mathematics standards or objectives from the district or state standards. The vocabulary included in state-mandated tests is aligned directly to the state curriculum; therefore, direct vocabulary instruction must focus on those terms to ensure student success on those assessments. More importantly, knowledge of these terms is the essential foundation for further mathematics conceptual understanding.

To further build students' mathematics vocabulary, invite parents to become their students' partners. By encouraging their children to talk about the new mathematics terms they are learning, parents give students more opportunities to practice their mathematical communication skills.

Effective vocabulary instruction gives students opportunities to communicate their observations and ideas, both in discussions and in writing. Math word walls provide a reference and reinforce students' understanding. Graphic organizers allow students to visually display the meanings of vocabulary terms and help students identify the similarities and differences of closely related or frequently confused concepts.

Students must revisit vocabulary terms. Repetition of the words or symbols in a variety of formats gives students practice in using vocabulary accurately in mathematical communication. Games and practice activities engage students in reviewing and "playing" with these words. Use mathematics-related children's literature to provide exposure to mathematical vocabulary in context.

Review and Reflect

1. Do you have a list of mathematical vocabulary terms aligned with your standards/objectives? If so, how was it compiled? If not, what can you do to develop one?

2. Why is it important to have parental support for mathematics vocabulary instruction? What have you done to involve parents in this process? Has parent involvement affected student learning? What further efforts can you make?

3. Think back on the strategies for teaching mathematical vocabulary described in this chapter. Which, if any, have you used in your classroom? Were they effective? Which do you plan to implement?

Chapter 3

Making Mathematical Connections

People are wired to search for ways to connect the new with the familiar. Even when we meet new people, initial conversation usually focuses on establishing links—either people we know in common, shared experiences, or mutual interests. Anything that helps us make a connection with our new acquaintance, that leads us to a better understanding of this person is sought.

In the same way, learning is intimately linked to the connections we make between our prior knowledge and our new experiences. Prior knowledge or experiences help learners interpret and construct meaning from newly introduced ideas or concepts. It is generally accepted that we understand something when we can see how it is connected to other things we know—that understanding is "characterized by the kinds of relationships or connections that have been constructed between ideas, facts, procedures, and so on" (Hiebert et al. 1997). As Hyde (2006) so clearly states, "Connections build conceptual understanding. The more and the stronger the connections are among related ideas, the deeper and richer the understanding of the concept."

In fact, according to Marzano (2004), research shows that "what students *already know* about the content is one of the strongest indicators of how well they will learn new information relative to the content." Furthermore, academic background knowledge has been shown to correlate with occupation and status later in life. Marzano stresses that schools and teachers can, and should, enhance students' academic background knowledge. And, since conceptual understanding is not "all or nothing," providing learning opportunities gives students a way to continually build upon and refine their existing background knowledge.

Making connections may be particularly important for students as they learn mathematics. Traditional mathematics teaching divided the school year into separate units of study organized around specific skills. After completing a unit, instruction moved on to a new unit with different skills, often unrelated to the previous unit. Many students came "to see mathematics as a fragmented, linear progression of skills like an unassembled puzzle" (Bamberger and Oberdorf 2007).

When students begin to recognize the mathematical connections not only within the discipline, but also to their lives and to other content areas, their understanding becomes deeper. Their lives are "enriched by deeply experiencing the *context* that surrounds the concept" (Hyde 2006). Instead of seeing discrete mathematical ideas as only colorful strands of yarn, somewhat interesting, but of no real significance, students begin to perceive mathematics as a rich tapestry of connected and interwoven threads intricately linked to their lives. Once this occurs, students recognize "mathematical connections in the rich interplay among mathematical topics, in contexts that relate mathematics to other subjects, and in their own interests and experiences" (NCTM 2000).

Making Connections to Enhance Learning

Students enter their classrooms at the beginning of the school year with an accumulated wealth of experiences, from in and out of school. Unfortunately, it is impossible for teachers to assess the extent of this amassed knowledge. In addition to wide variations in the amount of background knowledge they bring, there are also great differences in its content.

Furthermore, some students are exceptionally adroit at drawing upon their past learning, while others seem to be starting with a blank slate—sometimes because they have little to draw upon, but sometimes because they are simply unskilled at connecting their accumulated knowledge to their new learning experiences. So, while enhancing the academic background knowledge of students is beneficial, teachers must also explicitly teach learners how to recognize connections between their new learning and their existing background knowledge.

One of the behaviors identified by Fillingim and Barlow (2010) as characteristic of students who are internally-motivated, confident "doers" of mathematics is student-initiated connecting to previous material, distinct from connecting prompted by the teacher. These connections are often expressed in terms of "Hey, this is like when we…" or "This reminds me of…" Such statements clearly demonstrate the ability of students to make connections and extend their understanding of the concepts. As students identify the links between their existing experiences and new learning, their interest in and curiosity about the new content is piqued (Brummer and Macceca 2008). Since interested and curious students tend to be motivated learners, their learning is often boosted.

According to Bamberger and Oberdorf (2007), "seeking connections must become a habit of mind for students." Teachers should create lessons in which connections are abundant as well as model the process of examining concepts and problems for links through think-alouds. Mathematical discussions in which students share their thinking allow them to learn from each other. Teacher questions during these conversations can help students reflect on how ideas are related to earlier concepts learned or to future experiences. When teachers establish risk-free environments in which students are engaged and feel comfortable sharing their thoughts, students, based upon the connections they make and links to their prior knowledge, move from simply receiving information from teachers to assuming the responsibility of constructing their own understanding of mathematics.

Schema Theory

Prior knowledge is also referred to as schema. People continually build schema, or mental representations, of their experiences. Schema are the "sum total" of the background knowledge and experiences that learners bring to new learning encounters (Harvey and Goudvis 2007). Schema theory explains that all knowledge is organized into what are essentially "databases" in the brain (Brummer and Macceca 2008). New knowledge must be associated with and linked to the existing schema to be assimilated. The process of assimilation stores and transforms the new knowledge in the context of existing knowledge. This may alter the understanding of the existing knowledge. The more elaborate the schema, the richer the learning experience (Brummer and Macceca 2008). Without links to prior knowledge, the process of storing new knowledge is less efficient and less comprehensive. If new knowledge conflicts with prior knowledge, dissonance may result. To eliminate this dissonance, either the old or new knowledge is disregarded or restructured by the learner.

What kinds of prior knowledge or schema may students use to make connections? Kujawa and Huske (1995), when writing about reading comprehension, grouped prior knowledge into three categories: *attitudes*, *experiences*, and *knowledge*. These may easily be adapted to reflect prior knowledge brought to bear by students as they encounter new mathematical ideas or problems to solve.

Attitudes

Students develop attitudes about mathematics based on their previous experiences with it and, sometimes, based on parental attitudes toward math. According to Boaler (2008), "far too many students in America *hate* math and for many it is a source of anxiety and fear." While anxiety and fear about the discipline are not positive aspects of prior knowledge, allowing students to express their positive or negative attitudes provides teachers with insight. They can tailor instruction to address negative attitudes. Discussions about the attitudes some people have regarding mathematics can also allay the fears of students as they listen to comments by others who have more positive feelings.

Experiences

Students are frequently unaware of the many math-related experiences they have had until classroom discussions highlight them. Participating in tasks that require them to identify how their families used math the previous evening or keeping a "math at home" log focuses student attention on connections that previously passed unnoticed. Enlist parents to assist their children in recognizing the ways in which mathematics touches students' lives outside of school.

Knowledge

The knowledge students bring to their encounters with new mathematical concepts and ideas varies greatly from student to student. By encouraging students to relate the new knowledge to the old, teachers can enhance student understanding. Students may tap into knowledge about specific areas of mathematics, the structure of mathematical problems, problem-solving strategies, and any specific mathematical goals. Teachers can be instrumental in helping students understand academic goals, both short-term and long-term. When students aim at a target, they are much more likely to be successful in reaching it.

In the complex process of learning, students bring and apply their schema—the total of their background knowledge and experiences—in the process of constructing mathematical meaning. These previous experiences color every aspect of student learning and understanding (Harvey and Goudvis 2007). If students have nothing on which to hook new information, it is very difficult for them to construct new meaning. As Harvey and Goudvis (2007) so aptly describe it, connections to background knowledge provide "a bridge from the new to the known."

Proficient readers and proficient mathematicians use schema in similar ways, as shown in figure 3.1 (pages 90–91).

Fig. 3.1. Using Relevant Schema

Strategy	Proficient readers...	Proficient mathematicians...
Use schema to recall relevant prior information before, during, and after reading or solving problems.	• make text-to-self connections.	• make math-to-self connections.
Use schema to make sense of new information.	• store new information from reading with related information in memory.	• store new concepts and problem-solving strategies with related information in memory.
Assimilate new information into existing schema.	• make changes in schema to accommodate new information, thereby linking new understanding to stored knowledge.	• make changes in schema to accommodate new information, thereby linking new understanding to stored knowledge.
Adapt schema.	• delete inaccurate information, add to existing schema, and connect chunks of knowledge to other related knowledge, opinions, and ideas.	• delete inaccurate information, add to existing schema, and connect chunks of knowledge to other related knowledge, opinions, and ideas.
Articulate how schema is used to enhance comprehension.	• articulate in all forms of text and in all learning situations.	• articulate in all forms of mathematical contexts.

Fig. 3.1. Using Relevant Schema *(cont.)*

Strategy	Proficient readers...	Proficient mathematicians...
Capitalize on six types of schema when comprehending text and learning new material.	• use memories from experiences and emotions (text-to-self). • use specific topic knowledge (text-to-world). • use specific knowledge about themes, content, structure, and organization (text-to-text). • use knowledge of potential obstacles to comprehension (particularly in nonfiction text or text with unfamiliar content). • use knowledge about their own reading tendencies, preferences, and styles. • use specific knowledge about the author/illustrator and the tools he or she used to create meaning.	• use memories from experiences and emotions (math-to-self). • use specific knowledge about the mathematical topic as it relates to the world (math-to-world). • use specific knowledge about related mathematical concepts, problem structures, and problem-solving strategies (math-to-math). • use knowledge of potential obstacles to comprehension. • use knowledge about their own attitudes toward mathematics. • use specific knowledge about the mathematics domain and the strategies for creating meaning.
Use schema to activate comprehension strategies.	• monitor for meaning. • pose questions. • make predictions. • draw conclusions. • create mental images. • synthesize. • determine importance.	• monitor for meaning. • pose questions. • make predictions. • draw conclusions. • create mental images. • synthesize. • determine importance as they problem-solve.
Activate schema through sharing.	• learn by sharing with others.	• learn by sharing with others.
Build schema.	• receive assistance from teachers as they create background knowledge on a given topic, author, text structure, etc.	• receive help from teachers as they develop conceptual understanding and learn more problem-solving strategies.

(Adapted from Keene and Zimmermann 2007)

Kinds of Mathematical Connections

The connections learners use may be categorized by the kinds of schema they call upon. Readers may make text-to-self, text-to-text, and text-to-world connections. With text-to-self connections, readers make connections to their own lives. Text-to-text connections occur when readers notice similarities or links to other texts they have read. Finally, readers make text-to-world connections as they notice links to other subject areas, things in the real world, or phenomena around them. Likewise, mathematics learners make math-to-self, math-to-math, and math-to-world connections.

Math-to-Self Connections

Math-to-self connections occur when mathematicians notice connections between their own life experiences and mathematics. As students first begin to develop number sense, they may link the number five to their ages or to the number of fingers on one hand. When they work with money, their connections may relate to their allowances, how much a desired item costs, or how much money they brought to school to buy ice cream that day. Data collection and display may be connected with students tracking their progress toward academic self-set goals.

Older students may discover the mathematics they are learning links to computing interest on their car loans or the miles per gallon of gasoline used by their cars. When students identify mathematics in contexts that are meaningful for them, they more easily develop an understanding of these concepts. By leading students to recognize how mathematics is connected and relevant to their own experiences, teachers can take advantage of the fact that the initial mathematical knowledge of learners is generally organized around their own experiences rather than around abstract mathematical concepts (Hyde 2006).

Although these are some of the easiest connections for students, their ability to make connections is enhanced when teachers explicitly demonstrate how to make math-to-self connections as a strategy to help learners increase their understanding. Beginning with teacher think-alouds, students become aware of how to reflect on their own experiences to identify connections. Student interest increases as they recognize personal connections and begin to draw upon them to understand mathematics more deeply.

Math-to-Math Connections

Identifying math-to-math connections is more demanding of students than making math-to-self connections. Mathematicians, both experienced and nascent, make these connections when they discover links between their present and past study of mathematics concepts and procedures. Learners can draw upon schema about mathematical content, processes, and strategies previously encountered. Once they make these math-to-math connections, they can use their schema to explore similarities and differences between existing mathematical knowledge and new concepts, thereby enhancing their ability to solve problems and to construct new mathematical understanding.

In addition to providing modeling and think-alouds, teachers should plan lessons that allow students to participate in mathematical experiences where math-to-math connections become obvious to them. Using manipulatives may sometimes spur students to make these connections. Carefully crafted questions by the teacher can guide students' thinking so they become aware of these links. Additionally, teachers can provide experiences in which students encounter a familiar concept in a new and different context. Tasks that require students to apply preexisting mathematical knowledge to make a conjecture, to understand a new concept, or to solve a problem also help extend mathematical comprehension by establishing learning scenarios where students reflect and make math-to-math connections. All of these experiences support students as they build conceptual bridges extending their previous mathematical understanding to the understanding of new concepts and procedures.

Math-to-World Connections

Rich opportunities abound for teaching about math-to-world connections. An instructional focus on current events is a very effective way to highlight these connections. Mathematical current events are especially helpful for students who may not be exposed to news events at home. These events may be as diverse as news about weather-related disasters, elections, votes in Congress, sporting events, popularity of movies, or polling results.

As the class discusses important current events, teachers can help them recognize the many frequently unnoticed links to mathematics. Unless these math links are clearly expressed, many students continue to be oblivious to them. Teacher modeling and think-alouds show students how to make the links between mathematics and selected current events. Later, the teacher may challenge students to work together to find mathematical connections to the news events. Finally, students should independently begin to assume the responsibility of recognizing the mathematical connections within current events.

Math-to-world connections can be discussed anywhere in the curriculum. Anything read aloud may be a source of mathematics-related links if teachers are alert to these connections. Teachers should look for mathematics connections as they plan science, social studies, art, music, and physical education lessons. They can ask themselves these questions: What role does mathematics play within the grade-level curriculums for the subjects I teach? How can these mathematical links be highlighted within the lessons? How can students be encouraged to draw upon these connections to enhance their learning, both mathematical and nonmathematical?

The math-to-world connections are particularly valuable in leading students to recognize big ideas or themes related to mathematics. Students should be encouraged to consider: How does a new math experience fit within the larger scheme of mathematics as a part of our human existence? How necessary is its understanding to our lives? How and why did this understanding of mathematics develop? What did people do before it emerged? All of these questions encourage students to envision mathematics as a living discipline and to appreciate the important role mathematicians have played in history.

Teaching Students to Make Mathematical Connections

McGregor (2007) writes about making connections by describing the magic of a spider web:

"Spider webs are...magical. I gaze at them and think about the time and genius it took to create such masterpieces, works of art that go mainly unnoticed. What fascinates me is that these almost invisible connections link seemingly unrelated objects together. By early autumn in Ohio, you'll discover that almost everything outside is webbed together if you stop to notice."

Few of us notice or appreciate the beauty of spider webs. They tend to be ignored or brushed away until someone stops and points them out.

Too often, the wealth of mathematical connections students accumulate suffer the same fate as spider webs. In their haste to learn new mathematical material, many fail to slow down and draw upon rich connections to their previous experiences. But with scaffolding to support thoughtful reflection, students are able to call upon their background knowledge to make math-to-self, math-to-math, and math-to-world connections as they construct mathematical meaning and wrestle with mathematical problems.

Modeling and Think-Alouds

Teach students to understand and use comprehension strategies through modeling and think-alouds. It sounds easy enough, but to be done well it requires forethought and preparation. There must be a clear focus. To ensure that think-alouds sound genuine and conversational, Miller (2002) suggests:

- **Proper planning to prevent poor performance.** Although most teachers are capable of "winging it" if necessary, it is difficult to model the thinking involved when making mathematical connections without prior reflection. Before presenting a mathematical concept or problem, consider what mathematical connections can be made that generate interest and clarify thinking.

Construct a framework for thinking that students can emulate as they work with mathematical ideas. Will the connections be math-to-self, math-to-math, or math-to-world? Why is a connection of value? When will you describe the connection?

- **Authenticity matters.** Students love to hear about the experiences of their teachers. When studying area, if you are a pet owner, model a math-to-self connection about planning a dog run: How much area does the dog need? Is the size of the dog important to consider? That connection is relevant to the teacher and is, therefore, authentic.

  Or, share how area relates to a hobby like scrapbooking. A math-to-math connection might be modeled by explaining how to use a ruler to accurately measure the length of a side of a shape to determine how much paper is required to create the shape with a given area. Thinking aloud reminds students that linear measure is mathematically linked to the measurement of area.

  Make a math-to-world connections through newspaper articles, such as a description of the number of square miles impacted during a flood. The more specific and genuine the connections, the more impact they have on student learning.

- **Use precise language.** As you model and think aloud, use precise and concise mathematical language, particularly for mathematical connections, and be consistent with the use of the terms.

  Use the same set of sentence stems that leads to making connections, so that students become familiar with them and apply them automatically as they make connections. After several think-alouds, challenge the class to create a list of sentence stems that connect math to their prior knowledge:

  - I remember that…

  - This is just like when…

  - I know that…

  - This reminds me of…

  - That is similar to…

Some teachers may choose to make this a regular weekly stretch so that children form a habit of looking for mathematical connections to their lives. Others may use this method when introducing new concepts as a way of helping children tap their prior knowledge and experiences. In either case, it provides opportunities to explicitly teach the strategy of making connections while at the same time actually having students apply it, thus addressing the NCTM Connections Standard (2000) that states students will be able to "recognize and apply mathematics in contexts outside of mathematics."

Fig. 3.3. Sample How Did My Family Use Math Last Night? Stretch

How Did My Family Use Math Last Night?

Looked at the temperature T.R	1 2 3 4 5 6 7 8 9 B.A.
V.C.	My t-ball team scored 9 points. PG
Daddy bawt milk and got change back. L.R	My mom looked at the sped limit sign so she knew how fast to go. S.W.
Read a book and looked at the page numbers ML	Shared candies with three of my friends AC
My sister did her math homework. J.f	O.G.
5 5 5 DM	RQ

_____ **Makes Me Think Of… Stretch** (math-to-self, math-to-world, math-to-math connections)

As an activating strategy to introduce a new concept, students begin the day by recording the word or term that comes to mind when they think of the specified concept. For example, if the class is beginning a unit on percentage, the teacher writes on a large sheet of chart paper or on an interactive whiteboard, _____ *"Percentage* makes me think of…." Students write words that come to mind as they think of *percentage*. Each student is expected to record a word or phrase that has not already been recorded. In this stretch, only words are to be used—no numerals, pictures, or other representations (see figure 3.4).

Fig 3.4. Sample Makes Me Think Of… Stretch

Percentage **Makes Me Think Of…**

Finish this sentence above using words, numbers, or pictures. Add your initials.

stories on the news about elections
AM

100
MC

fifty percent
CM

a piece of pizza
TR

fractions!
PS

coupons at the market
LB

graphs
JA

the chance of rain
SD

ratios
SL

baseball and batting averages
OM

coupons
IR

Substitute *percentage* with grade-level appropriate mathematical terms. In kindergarten or early first grade, students may draw a simple picture and label it using their "best guess" spelling. Prior to introducing this morning stretch, it's important that young students be taught exactly what a *simple* drawing is through teacher modeling. Otherwise, this activity becomes too time consuming to use as a brief warm-up.

For each response posted, students make another connection—math-to-self, math-to-world, and math-to-math. In the ensuing large group discussion, as students share what they have written and explain why they chose their words, teachers highlight the value of making these connections and encourage students to use this strategy whenever they are engaged in mathematical work. Sparked by the comments of others, the discussion may lead some students to tap into prior knowledge they had not considered. This math stretch directly addresses the NCTM Connections Standard (2000) as it encourages students to recognize how mathematical ideas interconnect.

Mathematical Current Events

For many years, teachers have incorporated current events into their instruction. Even with the effects of the "testing" mandates, most educators and the general public still feel that students should receive a "well-rounded" education. For most, this means that students are informed about what's going on in the world today along with acquiring the knowledge mandated by the state curriculum.

Obviously, textbooks are a poor resource for teaching current events. To keep up-to-date about world news, teachers and students turn to the media. Teachers in the past frequently shared articles from newspapers or magazines or required students to bring in articles of interest. Some classes subscribed to weekly news magazines. With the technology revolution, teachers and students more often turn to the Internet to follow the news from around the world. Regardless of the source of information, current events instruction is an excellent way to lead students to make mathematical connections, particularly math-to-world connections.

Although it is not frequently a point of focus in current events instruction, math is relevant to much of the news reported by the media. In politics, the polls rely heavily on numbers. Understanding the state of the economy requires knowledge of math—unemployment percentages, inflation rates, the rising and falling of the stock market. Reports from wars include numbers of casualties, costs of the conflict, or related statistics. To report the effects of a drought, journalists rely on mathematical calculations to accompany their descriptions of conditions in the affected areas. Storm coverage includes precipitation amounts, flood levels, wind velocity, monetary damages, and numbers of people impacted. Sports coverage provides win/loss statistics, records set, averages, and news of salaries for athletes. Tables and graphs are often an integral part of news reports, organizing data so it can be easily assimilated by the public.

Our students live in a world where current events swirl around them unceasingly. Some students are only focused on those relevant to their own particular interests. A few are almost completely oblivious to world events. In spite of their level of awareness, for most students, math connections are rarely, if ever, recognized. When current events are included in math instruction, students become aware of the ever-present relationship of math to the world around them. Math becomes more meaningful and relevant. Students begin to notice how math impacts their lives in a multitude of ways. As this occurs, these connections offer teachers valuable opportunities to incorporate real-life math contexts into class investigations and problem-solving activities.

Math current events are not difficult to include in the morning routine. Dedicate a section of a bulletin board to current events. Initially, post math-related news articles and discuss them with the class, and think aloud describing how math helps to understand the article. Choose diverse articles to at first. As students begin to appreciate the role of math in the news, they can post and discuss articles. Commend students lavishly for contributing articles to the current-events board; it usually motivates others to do the same. If motivation wanes, consider awarding extra-credit when students share math-related current events or assign current events as homework.

Sharing Class Connections with Anchor Charts

As students assume greater responsibility for making mathematical connections, encourage them to brainstorm connections they have to connections to a mathematical concept or problem. Record them on anchor charts and display in the classroom for future reference.

As a third-grade class begins a study of multiplication, students might make the following connections:

- I remember that we worked on multiplication last year. We made arrays.

- That reminds me—my teacher said it is like repeated addition.

- My mom used it to find out how many hot dogs were in three packages. We were having a cookout.

- I remember how to write a multiplication problem: $3 \times 4 = 12$.

- It has to do with groups—how many groups? Remember how we made groups of counters?

- I heard on TV about the number of bugs multiplying this year because it has been warm and wet outside.

After the connections have been generated and recorded, teachers can challenge students to categorize and label them. Which are math-to-self connections? Math-to-math connections? Math-to-world connections? Time spent on this kind of categorization should be limited, however. The purpose of generating connections is the activation of prior connections and increasing interest by highlighting the relevance of the concepts to students' lives. Use of the strategy is the means to an end—not the learning goal. Ideally, this process of making connections becomes second nature and a strategy automatically used by students.

In the Context of Problem Solving

Many students struggle not only with the mathematics involved in solving problems, but also with making meaning of the written problem. Explicit instruction in comprehension strategies can strengthen the problem-solving abilities of these students. The first step in solving a problem is to understand it—what are the facts and what are students expected to find? It helps students to consider any connections they can make to the problem scenario. What experiences have they had and what do they already know that connects to the problem?

Primary students may be challenged with the following problem:

Farmer Lori put her animals in the barn for the night. Including her legs, there are 12 legs in the barn. What animals and how many of each could be in the barn?

The teacher conducts this think-aloud:

Whenever I read a problem, I want to be sure that I understand what information the problem gives me and what I need to find out. This problem involves a farmer and animals in a barn. I need to figure out what animals are in the barn and how many of each. How am I going to do that?

This problem reminds me of when I visited a farm last year. I saw lots of different kinds of animals there: ducks, dogs, horses, cows, pigs, and chickens. Dogs, horses, cows, and pigs each have four legs. Ducks and chickens only have two legs each. I just made math-to-self connections, didn't I? I know from my own experience what kind of animals are on a farm and how many legs each animal has. That helps me to better understand the problem.

The problem doesn't tell me what kinds of animals are in the barn, so I guess I have to decide. But, how am I going to figure out how many of each? It does tell me how many legs there are altogether. To figure it out, I have to put groups of legs together. That reminds me of something we do in math—addition. I think I have to add the number of legs on each animal to find out how many legs there are. Another connection! Did you notice how I just made a math-to-math connection? That connection is helping me figure out what I need to do to solve this problem.

So, let me see. I know two of the legs belong to the farmer. How many more are there? Oh—subtraction. Another math-to-math connection! If there are twelve legs in the barn and two belong to the farmer, I subtract two from twelve. Ten legs belong to the farm animals.

Fig. 3.5. Sample Circles of Connections Chart

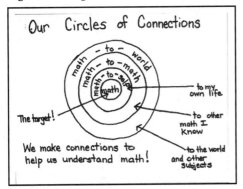

(Adapted from McGregor 2007)

Teachers can also make students aware of the difference between meaningful connections and distracting connections using a think-aloud. Just as teachers model the effective use of the strategy, they can model how they assess whether or not the connections will help them understand the mathematics concept or problem. This assessment should not be done as the strategy is first introduced, but later as students become adept at recognizing connections.

For instance, if a class is working with fractions, the teacher could think-aloud about their connections to this concept. One math-to-self connection that might be shared is "I can spell fractions!" The teacher may spell the word out loud a couple of times, and then pause to think. The think-aloud scenario might continue:

> *I am so distracted when I am thinking about how I can spell the word "fraction." Instead of focusing on what fractions are and why they are important, the letters just keep going through my head over and over. Sometimes the connections I make distract me from thinking about things that help me understand the math concepts. Let me just focus on what I know about fractions. I'm going to ignore that spelling connection.*
>
> *But, I'm thinking of another connection. I remember when we ordered pizza last week. The pizza was divided into eight*

pieces—each one was one-eighth of the whole pizza. Now that is a connection that is helping me understand fractions. I know that if a whole pizza is cut into eighths, there will be eight pieces. I wonder if it is cut into ten pieces, will each piece be a tenth? Do the pieces have to be the same size? This connection really makes me think about some questions that help me understand fractions!

Mathematicians, we have worked on making connections as we work with new math concepts or solve math problems. Don't let your thinking be distracted by links that won't help you understand. Whenever connections or links occur to you, consider whether they help you or distract you.

Later, students can be taught to use a Math Connections Chart (Appendix B) to remind them to focus on the meaningful connections. The chart has three columns, labeled as follows: *My Connections, Important to Me,* and *Important to Understanding the Math.* Students record their connections in the first column. They assess the relevance of the connection. *Is it something that is just important to me? Is it important to understanding the math?* They place a check under the appropriate column. Using this chart, students learn that their thinking is important and that they have the responsibility of monitoring the relative importance of their connections (Harvey and Goudvis 2007). These charts also serve as a method of formative assessment—letting teachers know if their students can distinguish between meaningful and distracting connections.

Encourage students to share their connections with partners, in small groups, or during whole-class discussions. Whenever they share, have them explain why they think their links are meaningful. How do these connections help them understand? Requiring this accountability as they make connections encourages students to self-monitor their use of this strategy with a focus on the goal of mathematical comprehension rather than on the generation of multiple connections. As an additional benefit of this accountability, students learn from and build upon the meaningful connections of their peers.

Chapter Snapshot

Teaching students how to make connections as they develop an understanding of mathematics concepts or apply their mathematics knowledge to problem solving can improve their comprehension and increase their overall interest in the study of mathematics. Their background knowledge becomes a foundation upon which new conceptual understandings are constructed. As they become aware of the relevance of mathematics to their everyday lives and to the world around them, students are more curious about and attentive to the nuances of this discipline.

With modeling and think-alouds, teachers can demonstrate how they make math-to-self, math-to-math, and math-to-world connections. Gradually, the responsibility for making connections is assumed by students—first as a class or in a group, then individually. Once students begin to recognize mathematical connections, they also need to learn how to distinguish meaningful connections from those that only distract them. The ability to self-monitor the value of the connections they make is crucial. It is a true indicator that students are focused on constructing meaning as they apply this strategy.

Review and Reflect

1. When we understand how to use a strategy, we can more successfully assist students in its application. Making connections is "second nature" to good problem solvers. Think back to a time you faced a real-life mathematical problem. What connections did you make that helped you solve the problem? How can this reflection assist you as you teach this strategy to your students?

2. How do you currently encourage students to activate their prior knowledge? What ideas from this chapter do you plan to use in your classroom? Why did you select those ideas? Once implemented, how do you plan to measure the success of those ideas?

Chapter 4

Increasing Comprehension by Asking Questions

Anyone who has spent time with young children can vouch for the fact that they seem to be hardwired for questions. It is hardly surprising since one of the most effective ways one learns is through questioning. This innate curiosity begins in infancy. Everything babies touch goes to their mouths to be explored. Because babies have not yet learned to focus on the "most important" things around them, their attention quickly shifts from objects, to noises, to activities, to people. They avidly take in sights, sounds, tastes, textures, and smells.

Although babies have not yet developed the verbal capacity to ask questions, their curiosity is obvious. As they grow older, their questions abound. Parents are sometimes overwhelmed by the whats, whys, whens, and hows with which they are bombarded. As Keene and Zimmermann (1997) write, "Questions lead children through the discovery of their world.... Children offer an endless stream of questions that delight us and drive us to distraction."

The Quality of Questioning in Classrooms

Most young children bring this enormous inquisitiveness with them as they begin school. They wonder about the world around them and seek answers. Most are willing to be "publicly curious" (McGregor 2007). As they progress through the elementary grades, however, something happens that quashes this curiosity. Even fourth- and fifth-graders begin to believe that asking questions displays a failing.

In middle and high school, the lack of curiosity displayed by students is even more pronounced. Tovani (2000) describes her dismay as she began teaching middle school: "Ten years of teaching elementary school haven't prepared me for such indifference.... Teenage apathy serves as a new roadblock to learning. Their refusal to nurture curiosity about anything school-related seems peculiar to secondary students." Postman (1995) aptly describes this change in student attitude: "Children enter school as question marks and come out as periods."

What causes this change? Some suggest that as students mature, they become more concerned about the images they project to their peers. If students equate asking questions with lack of knowledge, they hesitate to display their curiosity. Although this may be a factor, an examination of teaching practices indicates an additional reason for the decline in student inquisitiveness. Hyde (2006) suggests that "as students experience more and more schooling in math, and continually find teachers emphasizing the one right answer obtained quickly, they consciously or subconsciously think that asking questions is a sign of not knowing." Therefore, students become more intent on getting the right answers and not making mistakes.

Furthermore, Tovani (2000) explains how tempting it is for teachers to take over as *the* question asker. She spent hours crafting reading comprehension questions before realizing that she was doing the majority of the thinking, not her students. Asking high-level questions did not mean that she would get high-level answers in return. It became apparent to her that, "as long as my questions were the only ones that counted, I was going to be the only one interested in answering them." When the teacher is solely responsible for asking questions, students become disenfranchised. Students need to know that their questions matter and are valued. When students' questions drive instruction, students become more engaged and, as a result, learning is more rigorous. In addition, as they generate questions, students are practicing the habit of monitoring their own thinking. Are they confused? What do they wonder about? How can they find the answers to their questions?

The Relationship Between Questions and Learning

Keene and Zimmermann (2007) remind us that the root of *question* is *quest*. Enduring learning occurs as one embarks on quests to make sense of the world. In the real world, questions are at the heart of both teaching and learning (Harvey and Goudvis 2007). The acquisition of knowledge is driven by *real* questions—those that arise from curiosity about something and the desire to know more. Questions that do not have easily attained answers are sometimes the most worthwhile—in contrast to textbook questions that too frequently have "pat" answers. Queries that are not easily answered inspire interest and lead students to think more deeply.

The study of mathematics is constructed upon the questions and subsequent answers of mathematicians throughout history. When students recognize that questions inspired the development of the mathematical principles they are learning, they regard questions in a new light and view mathematics as a living discipline, rather than just a set of procedures from a textbook. Teachers have the responsibility to present mathematics to their students in just such a light. Rarely will students have this type of instruction outside of school.

Literacy teachers find that children who struggle with reading comprehension ask few questions as they read. In most instances, it is not the inability to *name* the words that prevents these students from understanding what they read. Rather it is their struggle to put the individual words together and make sense of them. In striking contrast are proficient readers who interact with the text by asking questions before, during, and after they read. Their questions lead them to make predictions, monitor their understanding, and, if necessary, reread for clarification. The process of generating questions is a strategy that allows these readers to construct meaning based on their own prior knowledge and the words of the text.

Similarly, the comprehension of mathematics concepts and problem solving by many students suffers from their lack of critical thinking and questioning. Questions such as *I wonder why…?*, *What if…?*, and *How can…?* lead students to examine what they know about a concept

117

or problem, what they need to know, and to extend their thinking. Instead of simply searching for key words or procedural shortcuts, when students generate questions about their mathematical work, it promotes deeper, more complex understandings.

When McGregor (2007) researched the value of questioning, she discovered M. J. Gelb's book, *How to Think Like Leonardo da Vinci* (1998). After reading the chapter, "Curiosita," she came to these realizations:

- Teachers can encourage kids to build on their natural curiosity by asking questions.

- The ability to ask questions can be developed.

- Sometimes there is no need for answers. In fact, sometimes there are no answers.

- Teachers should believe that the questions they ask influence the depth and quality of our thinking.

- It may be more important to find the right question than to find the right answer.

McGregor's interpretation of Gelb's reflections on curiosity and questioning as applied to teaching and learning is insightful. Whether students are engaged in reading or mathematics, their inquisitiveness and queries promote deeper understanding and enhance their problem-solving abilities.

Research has documented that as readers learn to generate questions, they become more engaged with the text. Through self-questioning, they are able to integrate the separate sections of their reading, resulting in increased comprehension and retention of the subject matter (Duke and Pearson 2002; Brummer and Macceca 2008). Furthermore, the National Reading Panel (2000) found that there is strong empirical and scientific evidence that teaching students to generate questions during reading benefits comprehension in terms of memory and answering text-based questions as well as integrating and identifying main ideas through summarization. Since self-questioning by students increases the comprehension and retention of the content, it is equally effective whether the text is fiction or nonfiction, whatever the subject

Students also need to learn that questioning is an ongoing process. Questions generated before the mathematical task help identify prior knowledge and guide students' approach to the task. Working with manipulatives to develop an understanding of a mathematical concept should be approached in a different way than the task of solving a problem. And another set of strategies may be used when searching for patterns on which conjectures can be based. During mathematical work, questions often arise spontaneously as mathematicians discover that they are missing needed information. After the work, questions may focus on whether or not their understanding or solution makes sense and whether they have, in fact, solved the problem. These types of queries are interwoven throughout mathematical work, some arising spontaneously, some resulting from more forethought and reflection.

Students tend to focus on spontaneous questions arising during their mathematical experiences. Teachers can lead their students to become more aware of the value of generating questions before, during, and after their mathematical work by modeling this strategy. By thinking aloud as they generate questions, teachers make explicit the process of reflection that inspires them to wonder. Going even further, they can explain precisely how asking questions before, during, and after their mathematical work increases their understanding of the mathematics. Students can then be given opportunities to work collaboratively to generate questions while working on shared mathematical tasks. After experiencing modeling and working together on guided and shared tasks, challenge students to use the strategy independently and encourage them to communicate their thinking by sharing with peers or by writing in a math journal.

Mathematicians ask questions for many reasons.

When students consider why mathematicians ask questions, it encourages them to use the strategy themselves. Some of these reasons can be explored during teacher modeling of the strategy. Others may be suggested by students if they are asked to brainstorm reasons for thinking of mathematical questions when they encounter new concepts or challenging problems. The class can create an anchor chart where students list reasons for asking questions. As additional reasons occur to students, write those reasons on the chart (see figure 4.1).

Fig. 4.1. Sample Student Brainstorm Anchor Chart

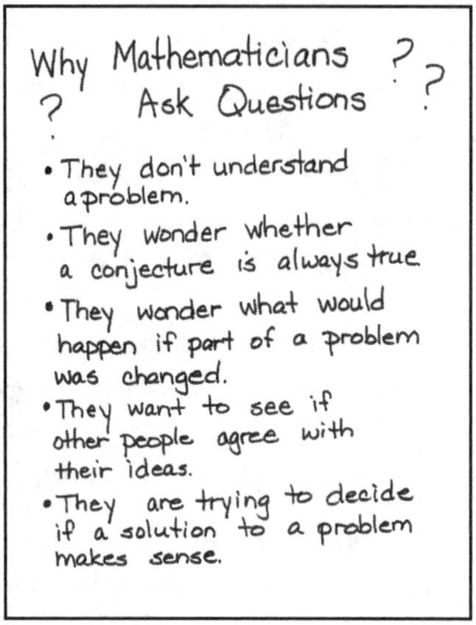

Why Mathematicians ? ?
? Ask Questions ? ?

- They don't understand a problem.
- They wonder whether a conjecture is always true
- They wonder what would happen if part of a problem was changed.
- They want to see if other people agree with their ideas.
- They are trying to decide if a solution to a problem makes sense.

During classroom mathematical conversations, encourage students to link their motivation for asking a particular question back to the reasons listed on the chart. Help students realize that asking questions is a strategy to increase understanding, with the goal being comprehension. By understanding the reasons for asking questions, students recognize when and why the strategy may be effectively employed. But, asking questions just for the sake of it is not the ultimate goal of instruction.

There are a variety of reasons for asking questions:

- **Clarification of meaning.** If mathematicians are unsure of a new concept or of a problem, questioning can lead to clarification. It may be necessary to reread, discuss their lack of understanding with others, explore the concept with manipulatives, or draw a diagram to help clarify the problem.

- **Increased engagement with the mathematics.** Questioning spurs both mathematicians and students to be more engaged with the concepts or tasks at hand. To answer questions they may have, mathematicians go back to re-examine and interact with the mathematics.

- **Critical assessment of the validity of the mathematics.** Questions can aid mathematicians in uncovering biases or factual inaccuracies in numerical materials. Additionally, when problem solvers routinely pause to reflect on whether their solutions make sense, errors are discovered and corrected. To be mathematically literate, students must develop the capacity to apply a critical eye to both their own mathematical work and the mathematical data they come across in the real world. Beginning in elementary school, students should be taught that data can be skewed or biased to persuade others or make a point. They can begin to learn how to actively assess data by asking questions, rather than passively accepting its truth (Whitin and Whitin 2011).

- **Monitoring understanding.** When mathematicians engage in the process of generating questions about mathematics, any gaps in understanding become apparent. When students apply this strategy, it not only makes them aware of gaps, but also assists them in plugging those gaps with the answers to their questions.

- **Identification of information needed for understanding or problem solving.** As mathematicians and students work to construct meaning of a new concept or solve a problem, it is important that they identify the key points and be aware of extraneous information. Carefully thought-out questions draw attention to the important facts and help identify the unimportant information—focusing attention on what needs to be known and understood.

- **Interest in and curiosity about the subject matter.** It is commonly known that when someone is extremely interested in something, he or she often has many questions about it. It is also often true that when mathematicians (both experienced and aspiring) are involved in the process of asking questions it takes them to a deeper understanding of the subject, and consequently they become more interested in it. They discover nuances that were invisible to them prior to the questioning process.

- **Extending understanding beyond the surface information.**
  Sometimes the initial exploration or problem piques the curiosity
  of mathematicians and leads them to wonder about concepts that
  extend beyond the original task. As a result, their thinking is
  extended. Synthesis of ideas occurs and that fosters new ideas.
  This kind of questioning has been responsible for mathematical
  discoveries throughout history.

**Mathematicians understand that there may be more than one
answer to a question. They do not stop thinking about a question
after they discover one right answer.**

In the traditional mathematics education that many of us experienced,
there was "one right answer" and only one right way to get to that right
answer. The teacher was the dispenser of knowledge. Students learned
that they would be successful if they ignored their own questions and
problem-solving strategies. Instead, success was obtained by listening
carefully and learning to carry out the procedures that would lead
them to the one right answer. If a student understood the meaning of
the concepts upon which the procedures were based, great! If not, that
was fine, too—as long as they were able to use the correct procedure
and to reach the one right answer.

It is odd that mathematics education evolved to this model when
one considers that mathematics grew from questions about the world
around us. Only through these questions did mathematicians begin
to discover the relationships upon which modern math is built.
Curiosity and questioning were crucial then, and they are crucial to
the profession of mathematics today.

Yet, most students still perceive math as a static subject found in
textbooks. Many students continue to believe that all math problems
have one correct answer determined by using one procedure (provided
by the teacher). When students begin to understand the value of
questioning and view the process of developing an understanding of
mathematical concepts to be as valuable as arriving at a correct answer,
their attitudes toward the field begin to shift.

One way of altering students' perceptions is to encourage them to
look for second or even third correct answers to questions. Too often,

student thinking ends when an answer is determined. To become more complex thinkers and problem solvers, students need to push their thinking even further. To reach a potential answer and then quit stymies the quest of students for deep conceptual understanding. As an added benefit, according to McGregor (2007), "Soliciting plural answers drives kids to generate deeper questions of their own." And, with deeper questions, richer, more comprehensive ideas are generated.

Mathematicians understand that many intriguing questions require further information or exploration.

Too often, the queries of young mathematicians extend only as far as the mathematical material or problem. Their questioning is framed by the limited context of the materials at hand. Teachers can expand their students' mathematical horizons by modeling the asking of questions that cannot be answered using resources that are readily available, but that requires further exploration. When teachers demonstrate the excitement of the intellectual challenge in seeking answers to these questions, it is infectious. Students, in turn, become more curious and eager to ask more intriguing questions and to go the extra mile in seeking answers.

It is important for young mathematicians to know that significant questions that arise from the true desire to know more and to probe deeper may not always have direct answers. These are the kinds of questions that inspire learners to linger over them (Keene and Zimmerman 2007). Rather than discouraging such questioning, teachers can create an environment of ongoing mathematical exploration and discovery by recognizing the validity and worth of such thinking.

Mathematicians understand that hearing the questions of others inspire new questions of their own. Listening to the answers of others can inspire new thinking.

Building a true community of learners is an important component of any mathematics class. Budding mathematicians should be secure in the knowledge that their questions matter and are valued. Questions of all kinds should be encouraged. The only exception would be questions that are asked simply to ask a question—not to find an answer or extend understanding. In fact, as Tovani (2000) so wisely points out, "There is such a thing as a dumb question. A dumb question is one that you already know the answer to."

Questions should be valued by teachers and by all members of the learning community. Bestowing value on the questions of all members is a demonstration of respect that makes others more willing to share their own wonderings without embarrassment. Furthermore, members need to appreciate the fact that by listening carefully to and considering both the questions and answers of others, their own mathematical thinking is enhanced.

Kinds of Questions

The process of generating questions results in a wide variety of questions. It is helpful for students to learn to categorize the kinds of questions they have about mathematics. It is often true that the questions that require more complex thinking are the ones that promote the deepest conceptual understanding.

Question Answer Relationships

One classification technique used for literacy instruction is Question Answer Relationships, or QAR (Raphael 1982). Using this technique, students classify questions as:

- **Right There:** These questions have answers that are literal, easy to find, and answered directly in a single sentence in the text.

- **Think and Search:** These questions are in the story, but are a little harder to find. The answer cannot be found in just one sentence. Readers have to think and search the text to find the answer.

- **On My Own:** These questions are not answered directly in the text. They require some inferential thinking. Readers have to think of the text and about what they know to determine an answer.

Although these strategies were intended for literacy instruction, they are valuable in mathematics instruction. Rather than learn a new approach, students adapt the strategy to a new discipline:

Right There

- *Conceptual questions:* If students are learning about division, they may have questions about the vocabulary terms for the parts of a division problem. This kind of question can easily be answered by consulting a Math Word Wall in the classroom or textbook glossary. The answer is straightforward and literal.

- *Problem-solving questions:* After reading a problem, a student may pose a question asking how many of a given object was specified in the problem. The student need only consult the written problem to find this literal answer.

Think and Search

- *Conceptual questions:* As division is introduced, a student may wonder in what kinds of situations division is used. By reviewing some of the introductory information and looking at some of the real-life problems that have been explored in class, he or she should be able to identify some of the situations in which division would be the operation used.

- *Problem-solving questions:* If a student has read a problem but has not yet put all the details together, he or she may wonder about the overall scenario described in the problem. By going back and rereading the problem, the student can gather the literal facts from the individual sentences. Then, the student uses those details to find the answer to his or her question.

On My Own

- *Conceptual questions:* Students may wonder how division is used in their lives or what other mathematical concepts are related to division. With these questions, students would have to draw on their own prior knowledge to find answers. In addition, questions that begin with "what would happen if...?" rely heavily on student predictions, inferences, and conclusions. They would be "on their own" as they come up with answers for those questions.

- *Problem-solving questions:* After confirming their understanding of the facts of a problem, students must decide how to solve the problem. Questions such as, "What strategies can I use to solve the problem?" require students to draw upon their own knowledge.

After a solution is found, students should always ask themselves, "Does this solution make sense?" Using the facts of the problem and their own mathematical knowledge, students are "on their own" as they consider this question. Other kinds of questions students may generate that fall within this category might include making slight variations to the problem, extending the problem, or increasing the complexity of the problem.

Thick and Thin Questions

Harvey and Goudvis (2007) recommend teaching students to distinguish between thick and thin questions. The thick questions "address large, universal concepts and often begin with Why? How come? I wonder? Or they address large content areas…. The answers to these questions are often long and involved and require further discussion and research."

Thin questions, on the other hand, are those asked to dispel confusion, to determine word meaning, or to assess content with simple literal questions. They are questions that can be answered simply—often with a yes, no, or a number. Although these questions are necessary, they do not tend to extend thinking or lead to increased critical thinking. When discussing the multiplication of a whole number by a fraction between zero and one, a thin question might be: Is the product greater than or less than the original number (the multiplicand)? The thick question related to this concept might be: Why is the product less than the original number? This second question requires that students be able to understand what is occurring with this operation rather than just the ability to compute the product and compare it to the multiplicand.

Because the thick questions engage students in a higher level of discourse, developing the capacity of students to generate and then attempt to answer these questions leads them to greater conceptual understanding. To this end, it is important that they be able to identify questions as either thick or thin. Teachers can model how to ask the two different kinds of questions and explain how they differ.

To visually differentiate between the two kinds of questions when creating a chart, record thick questions on 3" x 3" sticky notes and thin questions on skinny sticky flags (Harvey and Goudvis 2007). Or, use markers with wide or thin tips to record the thick and thin questions. Either way, frequently engage students in discussions about the differences between the two kinds of questions to ensure their understanding. By explicitly teaching students the value of the thick questions, they are encouraged to self-assess and then work to generate questions that lead toward deeper thinking and understanding.

Questions that Linger

Some of the most thought-provoking questions that students generate are those that are not quickly answered and that cause them to ponder. These questions are the ones that are capable of motivating students and instilling a fascination with the study of mathematics. Wise teachers take advantage of these lingering questions. Students are praised for the thinking that inspires these questions. The questions are posted and considered by all. Rather than providing quick answers to the questions, these teachers challenge their students to reflect, to write about them, to use the mathematical knowledge and strategies they have acquired, to discuss them with others, and to research them. Without the ongoing encouragement and interest of teachers, rich, student-generated questions are quickly forgotten and an invaluable learning opportunity is lost.

Teaching Students to Ask Meaningful Questions

The learning environment created by teachers can either nourish or starve the mathematical curiosity of their students. Tovani (2000) urges teachers, "If we teach our students to inquire, we will have a wealth of information from which to teach and our students will have a purpose for learning. It is our obligation to renew our students' curiosity and guide them toward inquiry." Creating an environment that spurs student curiosity about mathematics and teaches them how to generate mathematics-related questions increases student motivation, mathematical understanding, and problem-solving ability.

Modeling and Think-Alouds in Strategy Sessions

Teachers may choose to introduce the comprehension strategy of asking questions with small-group strategy sessions. Research indicates the value of teaching comprehension in such settings so that a teacher can initially explain and model comprehension strategies and then monitor the students as they apply the strategies independently (Block and Pressley 2007). (See figure 4.2.)

Teaching these strategies in a small-group setting has many benefits. As Fountas and Pinnell (2001) describe, "In the comfort and safety of a small group, students learn how to work with others, how to attend to shared information, and how to ask questions or ask for help." The intimacy of the small group encourages students, even those who may be reluctant in a larger group, to share their thoughts, so teachers can more precisely respond to their needs as they model and explicitly teach mathematical comprehension strategies (Sammons 2009). As students share their thinking, these conversations not only help them improve their mathematical communications skills, but also lead to more automatic application of the comprehension strategies they are practicing (Block and Pressley 2007).

In addition, since students may be flexibly and homogeneously grouped according to their instructional needs, the instructional content and mode may be differentiated. Because the small-group setting facilitates the teacher's ability to monitor behavior and attention, the instruction tends to be more effective at reaching all students. What may require 50 minutes of instruction in a large-group setting can often be accomplished in 15 or 20 minutes with a small group.

Fig. 4.2. Characteristics of a Strategy Session

> **A strategy session differs from a typical mathematics lesson. It provides:**
>
> - a time to consider approaches to increase mathematical understanding
> - an opportunity to examine the habits of mathematicians
> - a time for students to observe the teacher model, think aloud, and demonstrate the strategies used by mathematicians
> - an opportunity for explicit teaching that focuses not on a skill or procedure but on a strategy students can use in their mathematics work
> - a charge to return to independent mathematics work and apply what has been taught
> - a time when all students are treated as mathematicians and expected to use mathematical terminology and express their mathematical reasoning with precision

(Adapted from Keene and Zimmerman 2007)

Instructional time set aside for strategy sessions can be extremely effective. At the beginning of the year, teachers explain what makes a strategy session unique. Students should view this as a time for them as fledging mathematicians to learn about and reflect on the habits of successful mathematicians. During small-group sessions, students begin to consider themselves mathematicians and to value the important role of mathematicians.

Teachers focus on a strategy that students can apply to increase their understanding when engaged in mathematics-related tasks, and then explicitly model its use. As teachers think aloud, students are able to hear mathematical thoughts expressed precisely and pay attention to appropriate use of terminology. The session focus is always on a strategy, as opposed to teaching a skill, procedure, or mathematical short-cut. After several strategies have been introduced and students have begun to apply them independently, teachers may want to gather students together for a strategy session on applying several strategies at one time. In real life, strategies are seldom employed in isolation.

Throughout the session, students are treated respectfully as mathematicians. They are encouraged to explain their understanding of this new approach and to "try it out" with guidance from the teacher. Throughout the strategy session, students are expected to be a part of the ongoing mathematical conversation and use appropriate terminology. To conclude the session, the teacher summarizes the strategy and specifically links the newly learned strategy to the students' mathematical work. As mathematicians, they are expected to use this strategy whenever appropriate in their independent mathematical tasks.

Strategy Session Scenario

The teacher is meeting with a small group of students to introduce the comprehension strategy *Asking Questions*. The teacher notices six students who seem to be passive learners and chooses to work with them during this strategy session. The class has already been introduced to the concept of strategy sessions and is familiar with them.

> **Teacher:** *I am excited to share a new strategy with you today! I have a problem I have to solve tonight. The third grade met our goal for bringing items for the school's canned goods drive. I'm so proud of you! Now I have a problem: I told you I would bake cookies for the entire third grade and bring them in tomorrow if you met the goal. I need to figure out how many batches of cookies to make. To help me figure this out, I am going to use a strategy that mathematicians often use. I am going to think of some questions that may help me understand the problem and find a solution.*

The teacher displays a chart labeled *Questions about Baking Cookies for Third Grade* on an easel.

> **Teacher:** *So, I made this chart to help me keep track of my questions. I know that not every question I think of will help me solve the problem, but I think I will write them down and then eliminate those that won't help.*

As the teacher shares her thinking with the class, she records these questions on the chart:

- *What kind of cookies am I going to make?*

- *What kinds of cookies do most students like best?*

- *How many cookies does one batch make?*

- *How many students are there in third grade?*

- *Should I make them for teachers, too?*

- *What mathematics can I use to help me find a solution?*

- *Do I have all the groceries I need at home to make the cookies?*

Teacher: *That's a good start with the questions. Let me go back and think about them. I'm going to cross out the ones that I don't think will help me with a solution. I need to know what kind of cookie I'm going to make because not all recipes make the same number of cookies. But, I don't really need to know what kind students like best. I'm just going to make one that I have a recipe for. I'm going to cross that off the list. I do need to know how many cookies one batch makes—so I need to check my recipe. The next two questions are important, too. I have to know how many people will eat the cookies so I know how many I have to make. I also have to think about the math I know so I can solve this problem. That question stays. Next—the groceries at home? That's not going to help me figure out how many batches of cookies I need to make. I'm going to cross that off the list.*

From these questions, I realize that I need to know what kind of cookie I'm going to make so I know how many one batch makes. Then I need to know how many students and teachers are in third grade so I know how many cookies to bake. And I need to think about the math I will use. If I know that one batch makes a certain number of cookies, I can multiply to find out how many cookies are in two batches, three batches, or four batches. If I know that along with how many cookies I need, I will know how many batches of cookies to make.

Asking questions helped me identify the important information. I thought about the problem and listed all the questions I had that related to it. When I looked at the questions, I had to think about those that would not help me solve the problem. I crossed those out. This helped me focus on the important information I need to solve this problem.

Please turn to your partner and share what you have learned about asking questions to help you understand more about problems you have to solve.

The teacher listens as pairs of students share their understandings of the strategy. Several students were unclear about how to decide if the question was important to the solution of the problem or not, so the teacher makes a note to address this in another small-group lesson with those students and any others that might have the same difficulties.

Teacher: *Remember—whenever you are solving a problem, use the strategy of asking questions. This time I asked questions before actually solving the problem, but this strategy will also help as I try to solve it, and after I think I have found a solution. In your own work, be sure you consider this strategy to see if it helps you to better understand your problem.*

This scenario focuses on the introduction of a strategy to a small group of students. Additional modeling and think-alouds will be necessary to reinforce and extend the concept. Students need opportunities to apply the strategy independently as they work in small groups or individually, with guidance and specific feedback from the teacher.

Throughout the process of learning new comprehension strategies, it is crucial to give students opportunities to communicate their understanding. In this scenario, the student conversation was a "pair and share" talk. Student conversation was limited because the main focus of this strategy session was teacher modeling. Future instruction will encourage much more extensive conversation by students.

Generating Questions with Thinking Stems

Students are sometimes stumped when asked to generate questions about mathematics concepts or problems. As a mini-lesson, solicit thinking stems from students and list them on an anchor chart for future reference (McGregor 2007). Thinking stems that stimulate students' questions include:

- I wonder...

- Why does...

- What would happen if...

- How is this similar to...

- I don't understand...

- What other information is needed...

- What does this remind me of...

- What do I notice about...

- Are there any patterns...

- What strategies might I...

- What do I need to find out...

- Will diagrams, models, or other representations help me...

Throughout the year, as students become more proficient at generating questions, add more stems to the chart. In addition to kindling student curiosity, the chart is a constant reminder to students that asking questions is an effective strategy used by mathematicians and one that they should also use to increase their mathematical understanding.

Wonder Walls

Students may be encouraged to share their questions before, during, and after engaging in specific mathematical tasks by recording them on a chart titled "Wonder Wall" (Murphy 2010). Depending upon the grade level, teachers may record student questions, or students may record their own questions directly on the chart. Another option is the use of sticky notes. Students write a question on the sticky note and add it to the Wonder Wall chart.

The Wonder Wall chart may have a single column (similar to the chart created by the teacher in the strategy session scenario) or three columns labeled *Before, During,* and *After.* When students become more adept at the use of this strategy, the three-column chart provides added grist for discussion as students explore the use of questions in each of the three contexts. It is important that students interact with the chart beyond the process of adding questions. By sharing questions with their peers, the understanding of all students is extended, since one question tends to lead to another. The rich interplay of students' prior knowledge, questions, and construction of new knowledge promotes the deep understanding of mathematical concepts, which students need to confidently tackle mathematical challenges.

Question Journals

A more personal way for students to keep track of the questions they generate is the use of a Question Journal (Brummer and Macceca 2008). Each student receives a journal in which they record questions that occur to them during their mathematical work. Each sheet in the journal has four columns—one for *questions*; one for students to indicate if the question was generated *before, during, or after* their math task; one for a *predicted answer*; and one for a *final answer* (if one is found). (See figure 4.3 and Appendix C.) By recording possible answers, students are making predictions. Further exploration may prove or disprove the validity of the predicted answer.

Fig. 4.3. Question Journal

Question	Before, During, or After?	Predicted Answer	Final Answer

(Adapted from Brummer and Macecca 2008)

When Question Journals are used to record student questions, it is important that teachers read them on a regular basis. They provide valuable insight into student thinking. As you read student questions, predicted answers, and final answers, share specific written feedback with students.

Question Webs

Graphic organizers are used effectively in language arts instruction as a visual method of ordering ideas so that an overall theme or idea becomes evident. A Question Web promoting mathematics comprehension is equally effective and can be used in either of two ways.

In her classroom, Miller (2002) uses a Question Web to "help [students] and organize their thinking and learning in order to answer a specific question." The question is written within a circle in the middle of the page. Extending out from the circle are possible answers to the question. When the class or an individual student arrives at a conclusive answer, it is recorded at the bottom of the page. This type of Question Web can be very readily applied to mathematics questions of an inferential nature. For example, a primary class may wonder why standard units of measure were created (figure 4.4).

Fig. 4.4. Question Web

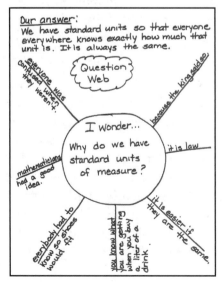

Question Webs may also be used to record questions generated about a given mathematics concept or problem. In this type of Question Web, the concept or problem is written in the circle in the center of the page. On lines extending out from the center of the circle are the questions generated by students. Alternatively, students can record their questions on sticky notes and place them around the center (figure 4.5).

Fig 4.5. Question Web for Questions

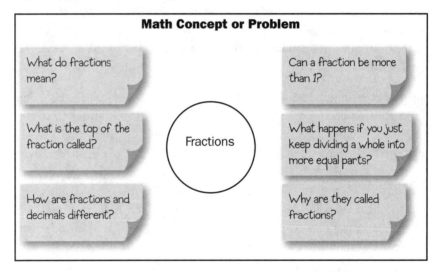

The discussions and thinking prompted by these graphic organizers enhance and extend the thinking of students. Teachers can facilitate the discourse, guiding it when needed with carefully crafted questions.

Math Stretches to Promote Questions

Using Math Stretch tasks (described in Chapter 3) to promote the strategy of asking questions can be tricky. Students should focus on *authentic* questions about which they are curious. It is difficult to design a stretch without encouraging students to come up with just any question solely for the sake of satisfying the teacher. For example, it seems as if the Question Web described previously could be turned into a good stretch. However, if some students have no questions about fractions and they already know the answers, they might simply add one to the chart or make up one in which they have no interest.

To prevent that, develop a Math Stretch that encourages students to reflect on a concept and think of questions that may help other students understand it more deeply. Lead students to understand that, for this stretch, they are responsible for reflecting on the concept to identify a possible area of confusion and then come up with a question to address it.

Questions for Understanding Stretch

Display the Questions for Understanding chart. Students should already be familiar with the strategy of asking questions to increase understanding. The concept upon which the stretch is focused should have already been introduced to the class. The chart directs students to "Think of a question that will help other students understand the concept of *fractions* and that is not already on the chart. Write it on a sticky note with your initials, and then add it to the chart." After all students have added a question to the chart, convene a Math Huddle to examine the questions. Students should be able to justify the question they posted by explaining how it will help other students better understand the concept..

The *Questions for Understanding Stretch* turns the table on students. In this task, they have to think like teachers. What aspects of the concept may be confusing to others? By examining the concept from other students' perspectives, they may discover areas that need clarification.

What's the Question? Stretch

This is another Math Stretch that encourages students to wonder during problem-solving tasks. A problem-solving scenario without a question is posted for students to read. The scenario should be complex enough so that students may wonder about a wide variety of things. For example:

Mrs. Hall's fifth-grade class is planning a party for their first-grade reading buddies. They plan to serve pizza and punch at the party.

The instructions direct students as follows: "On a sticky note, write a question related to this story that is not already on the chart, add your initials, and place the sticky note on the chart."

Student questions will vary. Responses may include: *Why are they having a party for the first-graders? How much pizza will they need? How much punch will they need? How many students are in the first-grade class? How many students are in the fifth-grade class? How much will it cost to provide pizza and punch? How much does one pizza cost? How many plates will they need?*

During the Math Huddle, encourage students to share their responses and the thinking behind the questions they posed. In addition, lead students to consider how the questions can help them understand the scenario more fully.

In the Context of Problem Solving

When attempting to solve a problem, students are often confused about what they need to determine and what information is necessary to solve the problem. Using the comprehension strategy of asking questions leads them to clarify both of these issues.

As students use the asking questions strategy to solve problems, they address the following questions immediately:

- What does the problem ask me to find?
- What do I know about this problem that will help me solve it?
- What information does the problem give me?
- What information do I need to know to find a solution?
- What strategies can I use to solve the problem?
- Does my answer make sense?

As students learn how to apply the strategy in problem-solving situations, create an anchor chart of possible generic questions that students may ask to determine the information needed to solve the problem. Use a graphic organizer to remind students of the importance of asking these questions as they solve problems. (See figure 4.6.)

Fig. 4.6. Questioning Graphic Organizer for Problem-Solving

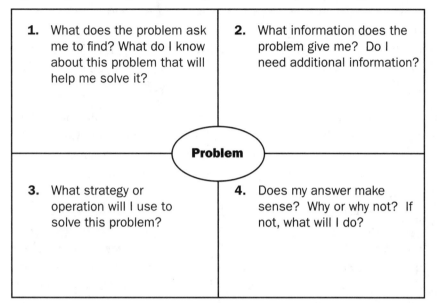

Using Children's Literature

There is a treasure trove of children's literature that teachers may draw upon to encourage mathematical questioning by their students. The titles of countless mathematics-related texts are questions. In fact, mathematical questions are the focus of many texts. Foremost in recent children's literature is the popular book by Scieszka and Smith (1995), *Math Curse*. The story follows the mathematical challenges of a student who, upon hearing her math teacher's statement, "You know, almost everything in life can be considered a math problem," becomes a "math lunatic" who suddenly recognizes math problems in every aspect of her life. This engaging tale is a popular read-aloud choice and prompts students to pose mathematics-related questions about the world around them. Through discussion and questioning, teachers can encourage students to become "math lunatics." Somewhat similar is the tale, *Counting on Frank* by Rod Clement (1991). The narrator of this story is a young man who is described as a "measuring maniac." He views the world around him in terms of measurement: *How many of his very large dog Frank would fit in his room? How tall and wide would he be if he put on every piece of clothing in his closet? How high does the toaster shoot the toast in the air?* His measurements, many of them estimates, fill the pages of the book. Most are presented without the questions that inspired the measurements. This allows teachers to challenge their students to think about what questions may have prompted his many measurements. As a bonus, the end of the book provides measurement problems for students to solve.

Finally, another example of math-related literature aimed at primary age students is *What Comes in 2's, 3's, & 4's?* by Suzanne Aker (1990). The content reinforces number sense as it examines everyday objects and also motivates students to be mathematically curious about their surroundings. While reading, students begin to notice how the questions lead them to make mathematical observations, just the way asking questions as a comprehension strategy can engender a deeper understanding of mathematics. When the connection between asking questions and increased understanding is explicitly examined and discussed by the class, students will be encouraged to ask their own questions to facilitate their understanding.

With almost any story, students can practice generating math-related questions. The humorous tale of *Stanley's Party* by Linda Bailey (2004) tells the story of a good dog gone "bad"—sleeping on the couch, taking food from the refrigerator, and having a party while his owners are out. Although in no way a math story, it can serve as a context for mathematical musings. Some questions may be very simple, others more complex. For instance, what time do you think Stanley's owners left each night if they came home at midnight? Why did you choose that time? If his owners left at eight o'clock each evening and returned at midnight, how long did Stanley have to enjoy himself before they returned? How do you think Stanley knew when they were about to return home? More complex questions might involve figuring out the number of dogs invited to the party. If Stanley invited five dogs to the party and each of them invited five dogs, how many dogs were invited? What if each of those dogs invited another five dogs, how many would that be?

Although teachers model how questions can be derived from literature, the goal of asking questions as a comprehension strategy is building the capacity of students to generate math-related questions. Student attempts should be praised and supported, but they should be held accountable to the texts on which they are basing their questions. If the questions stray from the content, teachers are responsible for providing appropriate feedback to help students develop relevant questions. After all, the intent of teaching students to ask questions when working with mathematical tasks is to help them increase their mathematical comprehension. Well-focused questioning helps students avoid misunderstandings and leads them to mathematical insights.

Chapter Snapshot

Questioning and learning are intricately linked. From infancy, people are curious and want to know about the world in which they live. Once they develop verbal skills, the curiosity is often expressed through questions. Because questioning can lead to greater understanding, it is one of the comprehension strategies that students can be taught and encouraged to use as they explore mathematical ideas and problems.

Teachers find that when children first enter school they are full of questions and curiosity. As they progress through school, however, their curiosity about academic matters begins to wane. Teachers often assume the role of questioners while students become passive learners. Students, when they are encouraged to wonder and to question, become more engaged in their learning. Teachers of mathematics can explicitly teach their students to generate mathematical questions as a strategy to help them clarify and extend their mathematical understanding.

Students who are expected to think, reflect, and ask questions about their mathematical work take increased responsibility for their learning. Because they monitor their mathematical understanding, they ask questions to help them clear up any confusion and to extend their learning as they probe new ideas. Developing these habits not only enhances students' academic success, but also prepares them for the future. As Block (2001) writes, "Good questions work on us, we don't work on them. They are not a project to be completed but a doorway opening onto a greater depth of understanding..." Only when students actively reflect and question is that doorway opened for them. It is the responsibility of educators to teach young learners how to use this strategy.

Review and Reflect

1. Consider a mathematical problem that you have had to solve in your life outside the classroom. What questions helped you solve it? How does reflecting on your own life by asking questions as a comprehension strategy enhance the effectiveness of your instruction as you teach this strategy to your students?

2. During one of your mathematics lessons, focus on the number of questions you ask and the number of questions your students ask. What did you notice?

3. How do you inspire mathematical curiosity in your students? How effective has this been? Are there any ideas in this chapter that you plan to implement? If so, why did you select those ideas?

Chapter 5

The Importance of Visualizing Mathematical Ideas

Literacy experts argue that the ability to create images and mental models is essential for reading comprehension, engagement, and reflection. In fact, according to Wilhelm (2004), "without visualization, students cannot comprehend, and reading cannot be said to be reading." Visualization occurs when readers are able to interpret the text in light of their own visual experiences. It requires not only an ability to decode the words in the text, but also the prior experiences that together with those words, enable the reader to produce mental images very much like movies in their minds (Harvey and Goudvis 2007).

In our society, we are surrounded by images, which most often are provided for us. In many of our pursuits, both leisure and work related, we tend to be passive viewers. Students are accustomed to spending hours with visual formats in the form of computer games, cartoons, movies, and television. In some ways, this familiarity can be an advantage in teaching students to use visualization as a comprehension strategy. They tend to be most comfortable in that realm. Because of their affinity for the visual, visualization is a natural fit for them (McGregor 2007). The drawback to the immersion of students into the world of the visual, however, is that these images are provided *for* them, requiring no effort on their part. They are thrust into the images visualized by others without ever going through the process of connecting text or mathematical experiences with their own background knowledge.

In contrast, when reading or engaging in mathematical activities, students must create their own visualizations. Educators must teach students to draw upon their own inner resources to generate mental images of what they read and the mathematics with which they work to strengthen their abilities to construct meaning. This process of meaning-making is unique because it is a product of the reader's own individual experiences. Creating mental images from prior experiences facilitates the ability of readers to organize and store new information by providing mental "pegs" on which to hang the memory for that information (Murphy 2010). When students visualize with automaticity, their comprehension is enhanced.

Purposefully meshing new information with prior visual experience in any content area boosts learning. Students who lack the ability to create these mental images often have difficulty with comprehension (Hibbing and Rankin-Erickson 2009). Most teachers can readily identify the characteristics of students who have not developed the ability to visualize the content of the text as they read. These students may seem unfocused or even inattentive and have weak auditory memory. When working with mathematics, they typically struggle with problem solving and responding appropriately to questions (Murphy 2010).

Visualization and Cognition

According to the dual coding theory of cognition, knowledge is dependent upon representation and processing by two modes, verbal (or linguistic) and nonverbal (or nonlinguistic). Knowledge, meaning, and memory acquired from reading or other learning experiences are explained by the representation and processing of information within and between the two codes. Rich verbal and nonverbal contexts together contribute to comprehension (Sadowski 2005). This dual process leads to the anchoring of new ideas in the permanent memory of learners (Marzano 2004).

Nonverbal interaction includes the representation and processing of objects and events based on one's knowledge of the world, or one's *schema*. The ability to self-generate imagery as a way of processing new information is one of the essential components of dual code processing. Whether in reading or in exploring mathematical concepts, learning is diminished if students cannot draw on both components involved.

What Students Need to Know about Visualization for Mathematical Comprehension

Just as proficient readers use visualization to make meaning as they read, proficient mathematicians employ visualization as they work to understand concepts and solve problems. Students need to understand the following ideas about the use of visualization by mathematicians:

1. Mathematicians purposefully and spontaneously generate mental images to enhance their understanding as they explore mathematical ideas. They know that visualization is integral to understanding.

2. Mathematicians draw upon their schema as they generate mental images of new mathematical ideas.

3. Mathematicians are motivated and engaged as they visualize mathematical concepts and problems.

4. Mathematicians continue to revise their mental images as they work and discover new mathematical information.

5. Mathematicians understand the value of sharing their mental images of mathematical ideas with others. They often adapt their own visualizations based on the mental images shared by their peers.

(Adapted from Wilhelm 2004 and Miller 2002)

Mathematicians purposefully and spontaneously generate mental images to enhance their understanding as they explore mathematical ideas. They know that visualization is integral to understanding.

Some young learners naturally form mental images as they interact with new information. Yet, studies show that most young readers do not spontaneously visualize as a reading strategy and are incapable of it even when prompted (Wilhelm 2004). If that is true for reading, mathematics teachers need to be concerned as well.

Explicit and direct instruction can help students recognize the value of this strategy. They understand that although it occurs spontaneously at times, it is something they can implement with intention. Student capacity for generating mental images is increased when they see modeling through think-alouds, and when they practice implementing the strategy with opportunities to verbally describe and share visualizations with others. It is imperative that modeling or sharing by students not only describe the mental images created, but also make clear in what ways the images improve mathematical understanding. It is easy for students to be so involved in creating and describing their visualizations that they fail to recognize the purpose driving the strategy.

Mathematicians draw upon their schema as they generate mental images of new mathematical ideas.

As with any discipline, when exploring new ideas, drawing upon prior experiences can enhance understanding. Visualization takes making connections to background knowledge a step further. What one already knows and understands is linked to new ideas and experiences to generate an image in one's mind. Without the foundation of an individual's schema, the image created is limited and the student founders.

Some students need to be taught to draw upon what they already know when trying to visualize new mathematical information. They tend to panic when they encounter new terms or concepts rather than pausing to reflect on what they already understand. Teachers can encourage reflection before attempts to visualize by including this kind of scenario in their think-alouds. Teachers can describe their initial alarm when coming upon a new mathematical concept and how they paused to think back to what they already know. Continuing to think aloud, they can explain how reflection enabled them to identify some connections between their prior knowledge and the new concept that they used to create a mental image. Students need to realize that the initial fear of not understanding a new experience is one that is common to learners, and that there are productive ways to work through that fear.

Mathematicians are motivated and engaged as they visualize mathematical concepts and problems.

Mathematicians are more engaged when they actively participate in the process of creating mental images. In order to create the images, they must interact with the new ideas, building upon and combining them with their prior knowledge. The challenge of learning a new concept or solving a problem becomes more approachable, less intimidating, and more interesting. As a result, students are often more motivated to pursue personal understanding.

Mathematicians continue to revise their mental images as their work leads them to discover new mathematical information.

During the process of exploring mathematics, whether learning new concepts, extending understanding of a concept, or solving problems, mathematicians often encounter new information that requires them to revise their mental images. Students need to learn the value of flexibility as they generate mental images. Rather than forming a vision and adhering rigidly to it, the accuracy of the mental model they visualize will be increased if students learn to pay close attention to additional information they discover and then adjust their mental image to accommodate it. This habit of thinking is one that many students need to be taught explicitly and encouraged to practice.

Mathematicians understand the value of sharing their mental images of mathematical ideas with others. They often adapt their own visualizations based on the mental images shared by others.

Learning is a social process. It is enhanced as students work with others exploring the same ideas (Van de Walle and Lovin 2006). Vygotsky (1978) stressed the importance of children verbally expressing their ideas in the process of reasoning for themselves. Not only does the process of verbalizing their mental images promote their reasoning and mathematical communication skills, but as students listen to the ideas of others, they are often motivated to rethink their original vision based on the mental images of their peers. This understanding also requires that learners flexibly create and revise their mental images of the mathematical ideas with which they are working.

Visualizing Multiple Representations of Mathematical Ideas

The NCTM Standards (2000) include representation as one of the Process Standards. The standard states that:

Instructional programs from prekindergarten through grade 12 should enable all students to:

- create and use representations to organize, record, and communicate mathematical ideas;

- select, apply, and translate among mathematical representations to solve problems;

- use representations to model and interpret physical, social, and mathematical phenomena.

For students to be able to represent mathematical ideas, they must first have a mental image of the concept or problem and be able to visualize it in the form of a representation. In fact, according to the NCTM (2000) the term *representation* includes both the process and product. If students lack the ability to create a mental image of the initial idea or *process*, the *product* will most likely be faulty or based on memorized procedures rather than true conceptual understanding.

Furthermore, it is important that students realize that the representations support understanding of mathematical concepts and relationships. Representations are essential in learning and engaging in mathematical thinking. By creating representations, students organize their thinking based upon the mathematical prior knowledge they have accumulated. When there are inconsistencies between the new information and their background knowledge, students find it necessary to reconcile the dissonance. The process that students go through in these instances helps them achieve a far greater understanding of the complexities of mathematics. Rather than remaining passive learners, they are actively engaged in the process of constructing meaning—the kind of meaning they are able to apply, retain, and build on.

As students first encounter new mathematical concepts, they should be encouraged to represent them in ways that make sense to them (NCTM 2000)—in other words, ways that are consistent with their previous experiences—even if these are not mathematically conventional. As their understanding progresses, however, it is important that they learn to create more conventional representations, to enhance their own mathematical understanding, but also to make mathematical communication with others possible. Students should learn to translate their mental images into mathematically appropriate representations. With practice, as with learning a new language, they can envision images in more conventional mathematical forms.

One of the complexities of visualizing representations of mathematical ideas is learning that a variety of representations may be required to support the understanding of a concept. Whereas students may first visualize fractions as pieces of pizza or sections of a candy bar, as their understanding expands they are also able to represent fractions as parts of a group, fraction bars, ratios, division, or as numbers (NCTM 2000). When their understanding and ability to visualize multiple representations evolves, students gain the capacity to determine which representations are most appropriate for any given purpose.

Building the Ability to Visualize from Words

The ability to visualize from a set of words, either when listening or reading, is important for learning in any subject area. Teachers should not assume that students spontaneously create mental images when listening to stories or while independently reading simple texts. Students who spend considerable amounts of time engaged in playing computer games or watching television (where the visual images are provided for them) often struggle to independently create mental images. These students need practice developing this skill in nonmathematical as well as mathematical contexts.

Wilhelm (2004) suggests a seven-step sequence of activities for students of all ages and grade levels who are not yet able to construct and sustain mental images of the words they hear or read.

1. **Create mental images of observed concrete objects.** This activity simply has students look at an object, and then close their eyes, create a mental image, and attempt to describe it. To relate this to mathematics, a student might be given a pattern block to look at and then be asked to describe his or her mental image. After describing their mental images, students open their eyes to look at the actual object and compare it to the image they visualized. Other students may add details or modifications to a particular verbal description. As students become more adept at visualization, ask them to look at several blocks together that form a design, and then visualize and describe it. Students are reminded that as they seek to understand a math concept or solve a problem, they can tap their memories of mathematical objects to help them generate new images that boost their understanding.

2. **Create elaborate mental images of imagined concrete objects.** Building on the visualization of concrete objects in Step 1, students create a mental image and describe an object they have previously seen, but that is not currently visible. This exercise prompts students to begin to retrieve images from their memory. Verbal clues can vary the characteristics of the object so that students develop flexibility in generating mental images based on new information.

3. **Envision familiar objects and settings from their own experience.** Students are asked to form mental images of objects and settings from home or other familiar places and then describe them. They can then illustrate their image with a drawing to take home for comparison with the original object.

4. **Add familiar actions and events, then relationships and settings.** Going beyond the visualization in Step 3, ask students to envision a familiar event or action, and then build on it. What happens next? Encourage students to describe the relationships among objects or to add motion to

the visualization to extend their capacity to visualize. Ask students to visualize a math problem scenario. For example, a student might visualize five warm chocolate chip cookies sitting on a plate in the kitchen. Then, the student imagines his sister eating two of them. He should be able to still mentally "see" the remaining three cookies on the plate. Perhaps he can even envision eating one or two himself!

5. **Picture characters, settings, details, and events while listening to a story read or told aloud.** Read aloud from texts that describe settings or events that are familiar to students, and periodically ask students to share their mental pictures. To link this to mathematics, choose vignettes on which to base mathematical problems. Students describe or draw images, and use these to help them solve the problem.

6. **Study text illustrations and use them to create internal images.** Together as a class, examine and discuss the illustrations from texts to add to the students' image inventory. Use math-related literature and math texts as well as fictional texts. By specifically considering the way in which mathematical concepts are represented in these materials, students establish a rich base of representations they can turn to when they create their own mental mathematical images.

7. **Create mental pictures independently.** Prompt students to employ visualization independently as they read or encounter new mathematical ideas and problems. Those who may be reluctant or lack confidence in their ability to create mental images can be encouraged to work with their peers or to describe their mental pictures in writings or drawings.

These steps lead students gradually through the process of learning to visualize and are easily adapted for use with mathematics. Once students become proficient at visualization, additional instruction is necessary to teach them how this technique can be used as a strategy to increase their mathematical comprehension.

Teaching Students the Strategy of Visualization for Mathematical Comprehension

Once students use visualization and have practiced creating mental images, they can appreciate its importance in understanding mathematical concepts and problems. The instructional suggestions described below can be used by teachers to increase the capacity of students to visualize in ways that enhance their mathematical comprehension.

Modeling and Think-Alouds

Just as with any strategy instruction, the most effective way to introduce the use of visualization is with teacher modeling and think-alouds. Students hear the thinking process behind the creation of mathematical mental models and their use to increase comprehension.

Teachers can use think-alouds for more than just introducing strategies (adapted from Wilhelm 2001). Depending upon the specific instructional needs of students, choose among these options:

- **Teacher does think-aloud; students listen.** This is the best way to use a think-aloud when introducing a strategy or concept. When teaching visualization, student attention should be focused on the teacher's explanation of the thinking behind the generation of the mental images. Going further, explicit explanations help students learn how mental images lead to greater understanding. Student participation at this stage of the process only distracts from the teaching point. Students should understand that this is a time of listening and thinking for them while the teacher has the floor.

- **Teacher does think-aloud; students help out.** Use this type of think-aloud after a strategy or concept has been introduced. Rarely will just one think-aloud lead to understanding by students. With this think-aloud technique, the teacher still carries the major responsibility for explaining his or her thinking, but students are encouraged to share their thinking during the process as well. With a limited amount of student engagement, teachers have an idea of how well the strategy or concept is understood. Student comments illuminate any misconceptions they may have after the initial teacher-only think-alouds, and errors can be corrected before they become engrained in student thinking.

- **Students do think-alouds as a large group; teacher and other students monitor and help.** Student think-alouds in a large group may occur in a Math Huddle when students gather together to discuss a Math Stretch, idea, or problem. Encourage students to share the strategies they used to help them understand their mathematical work more clearly and precisely. Prompt students to tell what strategy they used, describe their thinking in detail, and then tell how the strategy added to their understanding. At this point, all students are encouraged to be a part of monitoring the think-alouds of their peers through the use of thoughtful, focused questions, the kind previously modeled by the teacher. Student think-alouds during specific strategy instruction encourage student engagement, develop mathematical communication skills, and provide an excellent way to assess student understanding and identify instructional needs.

- **Students do think-alouds in a small group; teacher and other students monitor and help.** A small-group setting is one of the most conducive environments for student think-alouds. With or without the implementation of the Guided Math format, meeting occasionally with small groups of students with similar instructional needs helps focus on a mathematical comprehension strategy. Students are more comfortable in this setting and frequently more willing to share their thinking. Because of the size of the group, every student can be expected to participate and share his or her ideas.

- **Teacher or students conduct think-alouds orally, in writing, using pictures, or both; then, they compare with others.** Students may work individually and record their think-alouds in written form. Later, they can be given an opportunity to share and compare their thought processes as they employed a specific strategy with a given mathematical concept or problem. By hearing the thoughts that others are thinking as they apply the strategy, students expand their own thinking. In addition, students can critically (in a positive sense) assess the thinking of their peers. In some cases, as they reflect on the think-alouds of others, students will discover flaws in their own thinking. Alternatively, the teacher or student can record his or her thoughts in front of students, so the process of recording the visualization is modeled. This might be done on an interactive whiteboard or on an overhead projector. Many students need to see a variety of ways to record mental images before they are willing to attempt it themselves. Even those who are more confident learn from seeing how others represent the same mathematical ideas.

- **Students do think-alouds individually in a one-on-one conference with the teacher.** One of the most compelling reasons for one-on-one mathematical conferences between a teacher and a student is the opportunity for the teacher to get a glimpse of the student's thinking about mathematics and use of strategies to increase understanding and problem-solving ability. Encouraging students to show the procedures used to solve problems and to explain their thinking process shines a light on their misconceptions.

In the following scenario, the teacher has gathered together four students who are struggling with the concept of area. Previously, the teacher modeled with a think-aloud how to combine what he already knew with a new mathematical idea to create a mental image. For this think-aloud, he has chosen to encourage the students to help out as he describes his use of this strategy when working with the area of a rectangle.

> **Teacher:** *Today, we are thinking about area—specifically the area of a rectangle. Remember the other day I shared with the class the way I sometimes create an image or picture in my mind of something I am trying to understand? I'm going to use that strategy today, but I want your help, too. So, as I describe what I'm thinking, feel free to share any pictures or images you might have as we discuss these mathematical ideas.*
>
> *When I thought about the word "rectangle," I immediately pictured one in my mind.*
>
> **Micha:** *Me, too!*
>
> **Teacher:** *What did yours look like?*
>
> **Micha:** *It was very long and skinny.*

Tammy: *I saw one, too. Mine was more like a square though.*

Teacher: *That's okay. As long as your vision is a rectangle, each of ours can be different rectangles. Then, I thought about "area." The first thing I pictured is the tile floor in my kitchen. When we had the floor put down, we had to figure out the area of the floor to know how many tiles to buy. That's something I already know. But, then I put that together with my vision of a rectangle. I'm thinking of the area inside the rectangle now. Let me draw a representation of what I see in my mind.* (The teacher draws a rectangle with the interior divided into squares.) *I'm thinking of how area is measured in square units—just like the tiles on my floor.*

Sam: *My kitchen floor has tiles, too. Now, when I see the rectangle in my mind, it has lots of little squares inside it, too. If we count all the squares, we know the area of the rectangle.*

Teacher: *That's right, Sam!*

Micha: *That's how I see my rectangle! Just like the array we made when we learned about multiplication. I'll draw it.* (He draws a rectangle with two rows of 10 squares.)

Tammy: *It does look like the little tiles we used to make the arrays!*

Teacher: *You are really doing some great visualization. When you mentioned the arrays, it made me think of another way we can find area—other than just counting the squares.*

Sam: *Me, too! If we know how many rows and how many columns, we can multiply to find out how many squares there are. Looking at that rectangle with the little squares inside makes me think about multiplying. Is that why the book says that you can find area by multiplying the length times the width?*

Teacher: *What do you think? Does that make sense?*

Micha: *Hey, it does! That's why they have that in the book, isn't it! Is that always true?*

Tammy: *It has to be true. Look at our rectangles. Anytime you have a rectangle and mark it off into squares like tiles, you will have rows and columns so you can multiply to find out how many.*

Teacher: *When we took time and created mental pictures in our minds, it helped us understand why the formula for finding the area of a rectangle works. Mathematicians long ago visualized the same kinds of things that we just imagined. They used their images and representations to develop an algorithm that people can use to find area without drawing or using actual objects and then counting them. Remember that visualizing mathematical ideas is a strategy that you can use to help you understand new ideas or problems.*

The teacher began the think-aloud and encouraged students to join in. Once students were visualizing rectangles divided into rows of squares, the teacher prompted students to extend their thinking by suggesting that the image they described led them to think of an easier way to find out the number of square units without counting each of them. Students then connected their visualization with the work they had done creating arrays as they studied multiplication, thus leading them to the realization that they could multiply to find the area. Finally, students connected this to the formula for the area of a rectangle that they had read about in their math books. Since the object of the think-aloud was not just on helping students understand how to efficiently find the area of a rectangle, but also to learn how to use a comprehension strategy, the teacher concluded the small group lesson by explicitly describing the strategy and how it helped them understand this mathematical concept.

"Picture Walks" to Build Capacity to Visualize

One of the challenges of supporting students in their efforts to use visualization as a comprehension strategy is helping them build awareness of the variety of ways in which mathematical situations can be represented. It is impossible for students to visualize multiple representations of mathematical ideas and problems if they lack a detailed repertoire of images.

Providing opportunities to examine visual depictions of mathematical concepts builds the base of knowledge students need to create mental images of the concepts they encounter during their math work. The entire class or a small group of students can engage in a mathematical "picture walk" through a math textbook or other math-related book. Similar to the "picture walks" used in guided reading for primary students, this page-by-page examination of the diagrams and representations encourages students to focus on the meaning of each illustration and on why each image was selected to represent the mathematical idea. Students often fail to closely examine the mathematical illustrations in their textbooks unless expressly asked to do so. Model the thought processes involved during the "picture walks." Have students focus on the following questions to deepen their understanding of the use of representations:

- What mathematical idea is the visual depicting?

- What do the specific details of the visual represent?

- Why do you think the author chose to use this form of representation?

- How effectively does this representation promote greater understanding of the concept?

- Are there other ways that this concept or idea can be represented? What are they?

Taking a close, critical look at the types of representations in the texts gives students background knowledge they can draw upon as they independently construct mental pictures of new mathematical concepts or problems.

Visualize, Draw, and Share

This learning task builds upon the previous one. It requires that students have a familiarity with a variety of ways to represent mathematical thinking. With Visualize, Draw, and Share, they practice translating mathematical ideas expressed verbally into mental images, record those images, and then share them with their peers. This may be done in a large group, but it is most effective in a small group setting in which each student has an opportunity to explain the reasoning behind his or her representation.

For this task, students listen to a series of statements about a mathematical idea provided by the teacher. These ideas may range from something fairly simple to a more complex mathematical situation.

- I'm adding five plus three.

- Four-fifths

- The area of a triangle

- Prime and composite numbers

- Ms. Windham is having a party for 20 people. She has to purchase plastic cups that come in packages of eight. How many packages will she have to purchase?

- Mai has earned 10 dollars. She is making a trip to the dollar store to buy some gifts for her four friends. Each item at the store costs one dollar. There is no tax on these items. How will she spend her money?

Ask students to construct a visual image in their mind of each concept. They may use a method of illustrating the idea from books or create their own unique representation. When they have created a mental picture, they are given paper, markers, pencils, and other implements to record their images. Each student then shares his or her depiction of the concept, explaining the thinking behind the representation. Students may question and discuss the choices made by others. Then, assess the understanding of students and offer constructive feedback. The representations created may be displayed for future reference.

This task strengthens the ability of students to visualize mathematical ideas and create multiple representations by providing practice in translating verbal ideas into mental images and then recording them. In addition, their repertoire of methods to depict mathematical ideas is extended by seeing and hearing the work of other students. The discussions revolving around the student representations encourage students to critically consider the accuracy and efficacy of both their own representations and those of other students.

Multiple Representations Graphic Organizers

Once students have gained insights into multiple ways of visualizing mathematical concepts and problems, they can record their mental images on a graphic organizer. Not only is it important that students have the capacity to visualize mathematical ideas, but more specifically, they should be able to represent a given concept using mathematical symbols, with a model or diagram, with a real-life example, and with words.

The Multiple Representations Graphic Organizer (figure 5.1 and Appendix D), provides opportunities for students to describe, explain, and connect a concept or problem to other mathematical terms, symbols, procedures, and concepts (Thompson et al. 2008).

Fig. 5.1. Multiple Representations Graphic Organizer

Mathematical Symbols	Real-Life Example
Model or Diagram	Explain with Words

(Adapted from Thompson et al. 2008)

As indicated on the graphic organizer above, students fill in the upper-left box with a representation using mathematical symbols. The upper-right box should contain either a picture or a verbal description of a real-life example of the mathematical idea. Students draw a model or a diagram of the concept in the lower-left box. Finally, in the lower-right box, students write a description of the concept or idea in their own words. The completed graphic organizers may be shared in either small-group or whole-class settings to encourage students to consider additional ways concepts might be envisioned and represented. This work can be used as a means of assessing the ability of students to represent mathematical concepts in a variety of ways, but also of their understanding of the concept.

Math Stretches to Encourage Visualization

Brief Math Stretches can provide opportunities for students to practice visualizing mathematical ideas. There are two Math Stretch tasks in particular that help expand their thinking about mental representations. One focuses on different ways to represent a mathematical concept and the other on mathematical ideas or situations that might be the basis for a particular representation.

What do you visualize when you think about _____? Stretch

Display a poster with this question and fill in the blank. The question may read, "What do you visualize when you think about *addition*?" Students record their visualization of the concept on a sticky note and add it to the chart. They are asked to make their responses unique. A student might record two red circles and three blue circles with another circle around the entire group. Another representation may show a bird on a branch and two more flying down to land on the branch. Yet another may show an addition number sentence. Once all students have added a response, they participate in a Math Huddle, to discuss the many representations that have been added to the chart. This stretch allows students to expand their own thinking by seeing and hearing the ideas of others.

What does this representation mean to you? Stretch

This task is a reversal of the previous stretch. A visual image is illustrated on the chart. On sticky notes, students describe a mathematical concept, idea, or problem that the given model might represent. If the representation on the chart was an array of x's in two rows and three columns, a student response might be $2 \times 3 = 6$. Another may be, "There are two children. Each has three dollars. How much money do they have altogether?" Other responses might simply state, "multiplication," or, "repeated addition." As with any stretch, students discuss the responses in a Math Huddle, where they explain and justify their reasoning in mathematical terms.

Using Children's Literature

Some math-related children's literature directly connects mathematical concepts to real-life examples, thereby affording students the opportunity to visualize mathematical concepts in these settings. *Basketball Angles: Understanding Angles* (Wall 2009) uses basketball as a perfect backdrop for understanding angles (see figure 5.2). Taking advantage of the high level of student interest in this sport, the book describes angles and their impact on the game, while helping students visualize angles in real-life settings. Action photographs of players in the midst of a game are overlaid with diagrams of angles. The diagrams along with the verbal descriptions impress upon students how the angles in the movement of the ball or players are important aspects of the game. They will never look at the game in quite the same way.

Fig. 5.2. Children's Literature Sample

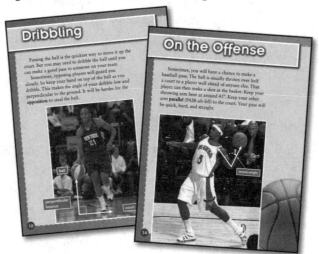

Poetry is full of imagery. The rhythm, rhyme, and often whimsical nature of the genre holds great appeal to children, especially if presented in an engaging way. These characteristics make poetry an excellent vehicle for encouraging students to visualize.

Introduce students to a poem every week. This provides an excellent way to teach visualization. Write the poem on chart paper or display it on an interactive whiteboard *without* illustrations.

On Monday, read the poem aloud to the class modeling fluency and conveying a sense of enjoyment during the reading. Then, invite students to join in the reading.

On Tuesday, focus on any vocabulary terms students may not know. If a poem is math-related, this is an ideal time to clarify any vocabulary specific to mathematics.

For Wednesday's reading, highlight a mathematics skill connected to the poem. For a poem with a pattern, focus attention on identifying the pattern.

On Thursday, include student interaction, perhaps through movements to go with certain verses or by asking boys to read one part and girls to read another.

The visualization practice occurs on Friday. Ask students to brainstorm how they visualize the poem. What mental images do they "see" when they read the poem? Once these have been discussed, students illustrate the poem in their own poetry books and take them home to share with their families.

Many poems have links to mathematical ideas. For example, the whimsical poem, "The Marrog" (Scriven 1979), describes a peculiar creature from Mars who has 17 fingers and toes, three eyes at the back of his head, five silver arms, and is seven feet tall. Keeping in mind the specific, detailed portrayal of this alien, students imagine how it must look and then accurately record that image in their poetry books. The enjoyable weekly experience of illustrating poems based on mental pictures they have conjured up enhances students' ability to visualize images and strengthens their skill at using visualization as a comprehension strategy when they are working with mathematical ideas.

36 Chapter Snapshot

Literacy research confirms that proficient learners spontaneously and purposefully create mental images as they engage in reading. Drawing upon their prior knowledge, these images help learners construct meaning from words in the texts they are reading. Similarly, mathematicians employ the same strategy to construct mathematical meaning as they encounter new ideas or work to solve problems.

The NCTM (2000) Process Standards call for students to be able to create multiple representations of mathematical ideas. Unless students develop the capacity to mentally imagine these representations, they struggle with this skill. Teachers can help build this capacity in students by modeling the use of visualization as a strategy to increase mathematical comprehension, explaining their thinking throughout the process. For students to be successful implementing this strategy independently, they need guided practice with timely feedback from teachers, and opportunities to acquire an awareness of the many kinds of representations used to illustrate or model mathematical concepts and situations. Furthermore, students have to realize that visualization is a strategy that may occur spontaneously, but it can be purposefully applied as they attempt to expand their understanding of mathematical ideas.

Review and Reflect

1. Consider a mathematical concept that you teach. How many different mental representations of that concept can you imagine? Reflect on how you acquired the ability to generate multiple representations.

2. How many of the representations that you generated do you think your students are capable of visualizing? Do you think a lack of background knowledge limits your students' capacity for visualization of mathematical concepts? How can you expand the ability of your students to visualize mathematical ideas?

Chapter 6

Making Inferences and Predictions

"Inference is a mosaic, a dazzling constellation of thinking processes, but the tiles available to form each mosaic are limited, circumscribed. There must be a fusion of words on the page—and the constraints of meaning they impose—and the experience and knowledge of the reader. In an inference, the whole is greater than the sum of the (literal) parts. Inferences result in the creation of personal meaning."

In this quote, Keene and Zimmerman (1997) describe a very complex process that most of us engage in every day, with barely a thought as to what we are doing. As we speak with others, we pay close attention and make inferences from their facial expressions. When a listener looks us in the eye and nods, we infer that he or she is interested and in agreement with us. On the other hand, if we see a listener's eyes flashing and cheeks growing red, we infer that our words are not being well-received. The imposed constraints on meaning are not the words on a page but the context of the conversation and the facial expressions of the listener. These inferences are derived from the fusion of the observed expressions and what the speaker knows about similar expressions from past experiences.

Although even very young children can infer the moods of their parents, many students find it difficult to transfer that skill to reading or working with mathematics. Yet, according to Harvey and Goudvis (2007), "Inferring is the bedrock of comprehension, not only in reading." The more adept students are at making reasonable, justifiable inferences, the better they are at identifying the most critical pieces of information (Brassell and Rasinski 2008). If students struggle to make credible inferences when engaged in reading or working in any content area, their comprehension suffers.

The Relationship between Inferences and Predictions

Inferences and predictions are closely related—both require that thinking and reflection extend beyond the given information in a text or problem. Both involve using background knowledge to enhance literal meaning. Proficient readers and mathematicians "read between the lines," as it is so frequently expressed, combining the clearly stated information with things that they already know in a seamless, seemingly effortless process to generate greater meaning. "Inferences are like lifting ideas out of a book and adding your own ideas to them" (Keene and Zimmerman 1997). By inferring, learners can:

- draw conclusions

- make reasonable predictions

- answer questions they have generated by combining background knowledge and explicitly provided information

- make connections between their conclusions and other knowledge or beliefs to extend or adapt that knowledge or those beliefs

- gain insight when struggling to understand complex concepts

- make critical or analytical judgments about texts or mathematical data

Predictions also involve linking given information with one's schema. A prediction is distinguished from an inference in that it describes something in the future that will occur—its accuracy can be checked. According to Hyde (2006), "A prediction is an inference with *attitude!*"

Inferring is an *inductive* process that requires learners to blend new information with existing knowledge, and then recognize a pattern or relationship that leads to the construction of new meaning. Teachers can and should help students develop their "capacity to *infer* patterns and then use these inferences to predict" (Hyde 2006). The process of making predictions goes a step further and is a *deductive* task—once a pattern has been inferred, learners test that inference by "*predicting subsequent manifestations of the pattern" (Hyde 2006). The cognitive processes involved are very similar no matter what kind of pattern is discerned (e.g., literary, numerical, visual, auditory, procedural). The strategy can be used effectively across the curriculum. When students learn to infer and predict as a literacy comprehension strategy, they can be encouraged to apply the same strategy when working with mathematical ideas.

Building the capacity of students to infer and predict in mathematics is even more essential than in reading instruction considering the fact that mathematics is a science of patterns. Recognizing patterns and relationships and then drawing inferences from them brings order and understanding to the diverse mathematical observations and ideas with which students and mathematicians work daily. Mathematical concepts emerge as ways of concisely describing these patterns and relationships. In fact, Hyde (2006) posits that every mathematical concept taught in elementary school is a pattern or relationship of some kind. Therefore, teachers boost their students' facility to understand and effectively work with mathematical ideas and tasks when they provide instruction that helps learners become more adroit at both inferring and predicting.

What Students Need to Know about Inferring and Predicting

All of us make inferences and predictions regularly, albeit subconsciously. For students to make inferences and predictions intentionally as a meaning-making strategy, however, they have to become aware of the process and of how and when to use it.

Students need to understand that mathematicians regularly use the strategy of inferring and predicting, much as readers do (Miller 2002). They should know that:

1. Mathematicians determine meanings of unknown words, concepts, and problems by using schema, paying attention to textual and graphic clues, rereading the concept or problem, and engaging in conversations with others.

2. Mathematicians use information from their mathematical work and their prior knowledge to make conjectures, to determine problem-solving methods, and to better comprehend the mathematical concepts with which they are engaged. They know that their inferences and predictions must be logically based on and supported by mathematical evidence.

3. Mathematicians make predictions about mathematical observations and problems and then confirm or contradict their predictions as they continue to examine their mathematical ideas and solve problems.

4. Mathematicians know to infer when the information they need is not expressly stated in problems, when they are examining mathematical data, or when they are grappling with unfamiliar mathematical ideas.

5. Mathematicians search for patterns and relationships in their mathematical work from which they can draw inferences to make sense of their mathematical work and exploration.

Mathematicians determine meanings of unknown words, concepts, and problems by using their schema, paying attention to textual and graphic clues, rereading or revisiting the math concept or problem, and engaging in conversations with others.

Making inferences and predictions is one of the strategies students can call upon to understand the mathematical ideas in their work. Making an inference requires considering new or unfamiliar information in light of what is already known. This strategy does not occur in isolation but is continually interwoven with other comprehension strategies as students construct meaning (Harvey and Goudvis 2007). To successfully make inferences and predictions, students *must* make connections to their schema, the foundation from which the inference and, consequently, new understanding grows.

For this strategy to be effective, students must not only rely upon making connections, but must take into account the mathematical information in their work. What is it that may be unstated, but becomes obvious when prior knowledge is tapped? What kind of patterns or relationships are evident that can be better explained when considered in the context of what they already know?

Students also need to be aware that they may need to revisit the new information to be sure they have interpreted it correctly. Was anything overlooked or misread? If there are conflicts between prior knowledge and the new mathematical information, how are they to be reconciled? It is important that students reread text or re-examine data or problems when they find inconsistencies. Modeling this step is essential this step in making valid, useful inferences and predictions.

Just as students are often reluctant to revisit reading or math explorations, they also fail to see that sharing their ideas with their peers is a method of reconciling conflicts and tapping into additional sources of information that could lead to well-founded inferences. Model how to consult with others and then explicitly show students how they revised their initial inferences based on the information gained through these mathematical conversations.

Mathematicians use information from their mathematical work or problems and their prior knowledge to make conjectures, to determine problem-solving methods, and to better comprehend the mathematical concepts with which they are engaged. They know that their inferences and predictions must be logically based on and supported by mathematical evidence.

Making inferences and predictions may go beyond providing an understanding of the meaning of a text, problem, or concept. As students observe patterns and relationships, they begin to think of rules or conjectures that might explain those patterns and allow them to predict outcomes in hypothetical scenarios.

Making inferences permits students to draw upon the array of problem-solving methods they have stored in their schema to determine which one best fits a given problem. As students explore mathematical concepts, by tapping their prior knowledge they can extend their understanding of a concept through inferences and predictions. Asking questions such as "What would happen if...?" and then making a prediction leads students to a new level of understanding.

Students must know that they need strong evidence for their inferences. The prior knowledge they are relying upon must be relevant and the inference must be grounded in the new mathematical information with which they are working—whether it be text, a problem, a concept, or numeric data.

Mathematicians make predictions about mathematical observations and problems and then confirm or contradict their predictions as they continue to examine their mathematical ideas and solve problems.

Inferences and predictions are rarely static. Students need to be aware that their predictions may be either confirmed or contradicted when they are checked. Not all valid predictions will be confirmed, and students should not expect confirmation of all of their mathematical predictions. Establish risk-free environments for students to engage in mathematical exploration so that they can freely make predictions. Help students understand that if a prediction is based on evidence, but is then contradicted, it provides mathematicians with important information. Students need to know that making predictions that are then either proved or disproved is a process mathematicians have used throughout history. It is through this exploratory process that new mathematical understandings arise.

Mathematicians know to infer when the information they need is not expressly stated in problems, when they are examining mathematical data, or when they are grappling with unfamiliar mathematical ideas.

When students first learn how to make inferences, they have little sense of when to use the strategy. They go on "inference and prediction binges." With practice and guidance, students begin to discriminate between when the use of this strategy is effective and when their efforts are wasted. Record the inferences and predictions students generate. As a follow-up, ask students to examine each inference to determine if it was of any value in increasing understanding and, if it was, what aspects made it valuable. These structured reflections will gradually show students how and when to use it effectively.

Generally, inferences and predictions are most effective for the following purposes:

- identifying specific information that is not explicitly stated

- creating conjectures or rules based on patterns or relationships observed in mathematical data or ideas

- constructing the meaning of a mathematical concept that has been difficult to understand

Have the class create a chart showing when using inferences has been effective and keep it posted as students learn the strategy.

Mathematicians search for patterns and relationships in their mathematical work from which they can draw inferences to make sense of their mathematical work and exploration.

Mathematicians are always searching for patterns and relationships in their work that can lead them to greater mathematical understanding. If students are encouraged to view themselves as mathematicians, they begin to place greater emphasis on their role in extending their own understanding of mathematics. Instead of seeing learning as simply receiving information from teachers, they understand that they have a significant part to play in constructing mathematical meaning. Central to the role of constructing meaning is their ability to recognize patterns and relationships, which they use to make predictions, and later, prove or disprove.

Building Student Ability to Infer and Predict

As mentioned earlier in the chapter, most students come to school already proficient at inferring and predicting in nonacademic situations. Most students have used clues from a television show to identify the "bad guy" and solve the crime. Many of the games students play require making inferences or predictions—and most students are quite good at this task. Unfortunately, the traditional mode of teaching in mathematics classes has discouraged students from thinking inferentially in the classroom.

When mathematical concepts are taught by teachers and then problems are assigned, versus using problems as a way to teach concepts and build conceptual understanding, students have few opportunities to practice thinking inferentially about mathematics. When problems with only one correct solution are assigned and only one method of solving the problem is accepted, students are discouraged from thinking inferentially. Students learn to simply shut down that mode of thinking.

In classrooms where students are expected to assume a major role in their own learning, they are encouraged to go beyond the literal mathematical information they encounter. This may confuse students who have seldom been called upon to use these skills. You may have to explicitly teach students how to effectively use inferences and predictions as a strategy to better understand math.

Just as with learning to read, repetition is important in developing a student's capacity to infer and predict. Beginning readers love to reread familiar books. Because of their familiarity with the texts, repeated readings allow youngsters to accurately predict what will come next in the story—and they delight in that ability.

Learning to make valid inferences and predictions takes time and practice. According to Hyde (2006), "It comes from many examples and kids perceiving the patterns. They need to see, hear, and touch the patterns to fully understand them. Then they can use the patterns to predict and that makes them feel confident and even powerful." Through repeated exposure and by encouraging students to explain their thinking as they go, they gain confidence in their ability to make inferences and begin to feel mathematically empowered.

As students work with mathematical ideas, they need to develop the ability to delineate between literal thinking and inferential thinking (Murphy 2010). This distinction has traditionally been taught during reading instruction; however, students need to be aware of how critical these distinctions are in other subject areas as well. Students should know that literal questions can be answered from information that is "right there" and clearly stated, while inferential questions require references to one's own prior knowledge.

Many students have difficulty distinguishing between these two types of questions. When they subconsciously make inferences, learners sometimes believe these ideas to be literal information. Errors of this kind can lead to mathematical misconceptions and problem-solving mistakes. Students need to be metacognitively aware because inferences must be checked for accuracy (Hyde 2006). If students implicitly accept their inferences as literal facts, they often wind up working with erroneous information. Teachers can lead students to consider the origins of the information they are using in their mathematical work. Explicitly model the internal thought process about deciding what literal information comes from the mathematics with which you are working and which information is inferred.

Making inferences is often a challenge, especially for struggling students. Because traditional instructional methods discouraged this process, many students lack the knowledge to generate inferences. Whenever teachers provide opportunities for students to gain background knowledge, they indirectly increase the capacity of students to infer and predict.

Teachers can enrich the background knowledge that all students bring to the process of inferring through the use of concrete representations as concepts and problems are introduced (Hyde 2006). Visual, hands-on experiences add to students' reservoirs of background knowledge. Then, once students begin to internalize the meanings represented by the concrete representations, they progress to the use of more symbolic or abstract representations. The accumulation of experiences they garner adds to their ability to make inferences from problems or new concepts.

Inferring Requires Time for Reflection

We live in a world where time is precious. Teachers hold themselves accountable for the academic success of each of their students. Some students arrive in class prepared for the grade-level mathematics curriculum; others arrive woefully unprepared. Yet, in only one short academic year, teachers must move students through ever more challenging curriculums. No wonder teachers are so often harried.

In striking contrast to the pressure on teachers to "hurry, hurry, hurry" through the mandated standards is the knowledge that learning requires time and reflection. Keene and Zimmerman (2007) describe a "lasting-lessons-for-teaching" realization: "…we should work to create an ethic in the classroom that values longer periods of time for reflection, not just on inference, but on all the strategies and across the curriculum…. When we create a norm that values time for reflection, children quickly adapt to that norm and become accustomed to taking time to think more deeply."

Because the process of inferring requires that students cognitively delve into their earlier learning, inferences do not come easily. They need to be given sufficient time and encouragement to rummage through their accumulated mathematical knowledge so they are able to identify those ideas that can be linked with the new mathematical information to create an inference or prediction. They may also need prompts. Ask high-level, inferential questions to encourage students to reflect and activate their prior knowledge. As a result, they will be better able to recall and understand concepts and content (Duke and Pearson 2002).

One-on-One Conferences to Promote Effective Inferences and Predictions

Think-alouds allows students access to the thoughts of their teachers. To truly meet the needs of students, you must access their thoughts as well. One-on-one conferences provide a portal into student thinking. Keene and Zimmerman (2007) go so far as to refer to conferences as the "lifeblood to comprehension teaching." Focused conversations with individual students allow you to see each student's strengths and weaknesses. These insights allow you to specifically identify the instructional needs of each student and to address these needs in the conference or through small-group instruction.

Conferring with students is especially useful when helping students improve their abilities to infer and predict. To become competent at inferring, students must determine which parts of their prior knowledge are linked to their immediate mathematical work and will assist them in making an inference. Students must identify and then knit relevant prior knowledge with their new mathematical information, combining them to produce enhanced understanding. This is a very complex process.

Misconceptions frequently arise from very logical inferences. For instance, students may infer that the area of circles cannot be measured in *square* units since it is circular, or that there are no numbers between zero and one since they do not use them in counting objects. Even when students are logically inferring and predicting based on their background knowledge, their inferences may lead to misconceptions (Bamberger, Oberdorf, and Schultz-Ferrell 2010). One-on-one conferences help get to the root of these misconceptions.

Assessing students' efforts at inferring is an almost impossible task unless teachers are able to gain insight into their thinking. The intimate nature of a one-on-one conference makes students comfortable and willing to share their thinking. Tailor questions and comments specifically to the individual student. With a few targeted questions, you can identify what a student is doing well and identify a teaching point. What will help this student improve his or her skill at inferring and predicting? Always include an authentic compliment for the student, acknowledging an identified strength. Then briefly share the "next step" instructionally. If more intensive instruction is necessary, include the student in a small-group session to address the identified teaching point (Sammons 2009; Calkins 1994; Calkins 2000; Keene and Zimmerman 2007).

Burns (2010) emphasizes the importance of one-on-one conferences with students, warning that too often teachers probe student thinking only when they answer incorrectly. Missing from mathematics instruction is the opportunity to learn how all students are reasoning as they are learning mathematics. If students are not asked to explain their reasoning, it is impossible to be sure how they are reasoning or what they understand. Burns advises teachers:

 **"We know that the students in our classes have a range of mathematical skills, understanding, intuition, interests, approaches to learning, and needs. The more information we have about them, the better prepared we are to make effective instruction decisions. The challenge is to balance the teaching of math with the teaching of students. Talking to students one-on-one can help teachers find that balance."**

Teaching Students to Infer and Predict to Enhance Mathematical Understanding

Explicit instruction helps students become more agile in inferring and predicting. First, lead students to see how they already use this skill daily, and then show them how they can apply the same skill to help them understand new mathematical concepts and problems.

Modeling and Think-Alouds

Many students, especially those who struggle, come to regard mathematics as something formidable. To some, it appears to be a discipline that makes no sense and requires them to memorize rules, procedures, and facts. This image is hardly enticing. As a result, too many are reluctant to think deeply about mathematical concepts and shut down when challenged to solve mathematical problems. Unfortunately, there is a common misconception that mathematics achievement is due almost solely to ability rather than effort.

Research shows that students' beliefs about learning are related to their mathematics performance (U.S. Department of Education 2008). Luckily, students' beliefs can be changed. Modeling and think-alouds by teachers are ways in which students can come to recognize that even teachers sometimes wrestle with solving mathematical problems and understanding new math concepts—and that even teachers sometimes make mathematical errors. With think-alouds students hear the thoughts of a teacher as he or she grapples with a problem or concept. Using these techniques, teachers lead students to the realization that mathematical understanding does not always come easily and that effort makes a difference.

When skillfully presented, modeling and think-alouds can help students in the following ways:

- Students understand that mathematics makes sense. More than the process of memorization, mathematics is a set of patterns and relationships on which concepts are built.

- Students move beyond a literal interpretation of mathematics to a more inferential understanding. Students begin to recognize how concepts are linked.

- Students learn to employ a collection of strategies for comprehension and for problem solving.

- Students recognize when particular strategies are most effectively applied.

- Students share the perspective and outlook of one who has been successful.

- Students internalize the mathematical way of approaching new information and problem solving. They recognize the need to mentally wrestle with problems and new ideas and abandon the expectation of passively acquiring knowledge. And, at times, they come to relish this mental engagement.

When modeling the use of inferences, bear in mind that students already implement this strategy daily without much thought. Plan to model the kind of inference or prediction with which students are already familiar before moving on to one more directly linked to mathematics. For example, share a real-life experience where making an inference led to a prediction:

> I want to share something that happened to me the other day. When I got home and walked in the door, I was puzzled. Usually, my dog comes bounding up to greet me, wagging his tail. But there was no greeting. In fact, I didn't even see my dog. When I finally found my dog in the den, he walked over to greet me, but he was hanging his head. His tail was tucked between his legs, and he seemed to cower. I wondered why he was acting so strangely. I thought of times when he had behaved that way before. Once, he had dug through the kitchen garbage can. When I scolded him, he hung his head and tail and cowered. I thought, "Uh-oh, I had better check the garbage." Sure enough, he had been in the garbage again.

As I thought about how my dog was behaving and then thought back to other times he had acted in the same way, I was making an inference. To help explain my dog's behavior, I thought back to a prior experience and predicted that I would find the garbage strewn around the kitchen. Has anything similar ever happened to you?

When we infer, it helps us to understand new information— not only in situations like I described, but also when we work with math. We will be talking more about inferences and predictions and how we can use them as we work with mathematics.

A brief think-aloud familiarizes students with the concept of making inferences by sharing a common experience with which they can relate. Building on that foundation, instruction will target how the strategy can be applied to mathematics.

After second-grade students have had an opportunity to explore addition problems requiring regrouping, use this teacher think-aloud focused on using inferring and predicting as a comprehension strategy when adding 25 + 17.

Okay. I need to add 25 and 17. Let me write 25. I'll put the 17 just below it. I think I will try adding the ones first. 5 plus 7 equals 12. Good. I'll write it under the 7.

$$\begin{array}{r} 25 \\ +17 \\ \hline 12 \end{array}$$

Now I will add the 2 and the 1. That's 3. So I will write it below, too.

$$\begin{array}{r} 25 \\ +17 \\ \hline 312 \end{array}$$

So, the sum is 312. Wait, that doesn't make sense. That's way too much. That can't be right, can it? 20 plus 10 would only be 30. Let me think about this some more.

I wonder if there's something about tens and ones that might help me understand this. Twelve is one ten and two ones. Okay so far. The 1 is in the tens place and the 2 is in the ones place.

Now when I add 2 and 1—but, no! I'm not really adding 2 and 1. They are in the tens place, so I'm adding 20 and 10. That's 30. So, there should be a 3 in the tens place. But it's not in the tens place, it's in the hundreds place. That's not right!

I really have one ten from adding 5 and 7 and three more tens from adding 20 and 10. I think I need to add the tens together. I should have four tens. I am going to change my answer. It should be 42.

$$\begin{array}{r} 25 \\ +17 \\ \hline 42 \end{array}$$

Wow! I am glad I went back and thought about this. When I thought about my answer, I knew it didn't make sense. First, I used what I already know about the value of these two numbers and predicted that the answer would be closer to thirty. Then I had to figure out what I did wrong. Sometimes, if I am confused, I try to think back to something I already know that might help me figure it out. This time, I thought about what I already know about place value. Instead of just thinking that I had a 3, a 1, and a 2 in my answer, I inferred that what I really had was three tens, one ten, and two ones, and then I predicted that I would have to add the tens together and write them in the tens place. That answer makes sense. I understand this much better now!

If you don't understand the math, you can use the strategy of making inferences or predictions. Think about the problem and then think back to what you already know. Often, when you put the two together, you can better understand the new information. As mathematicians, be sure to remember and use this valuable strategy.

In this scenario, the teacher was conducting a think-aloud focused on a problem students had grappled with the previous day. The think-aloud was all the more engaging to the students because they had experienced similar dilemmas as they attempted to add double-digit numbers.

Word Splash

As students become more adroit at recognizing patterns and similarities, their ability to generalize and make predictions also improves. With a Word Splash, students are asked to discover how words are related so they can predict the topic of study. This activity provides valuable practice making inferences and at the same time is a very effective activating strategy as students tap their prior knowledge about the introduction of new mathematical content.

To prepare a Word Splash, choose key words or expressions related to a concept or topic. Display these words and have students try to determine what common thread connects them. Jot down students' ideas on a chart to give an overall visual summary. As students share their ideas, they should provide evidence to support their reasoning. (See figure 6.1.)

Fig. 6.1. Word Splash to Introduce a Unit on Fractions

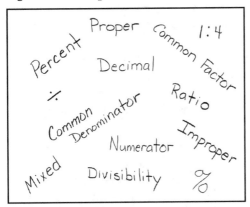

Inference and Evidence

When teaching students to infer, McGregor (2007) uses a two-column chart to record student inferences and their evidence for making the inference. This device teaches students that inferences are not wild guesses, but instead are based on evidence from exploring the concepts or problems and from their prior knowledge.

Students need to be held accountable for making inferences based on facts and knowledge. This requires effort, and initially, some students may be reluctant to make the effort to thoughtfully examine ideas in light of their own prior knowledge. Once they understand that they are expected to justify their inferences, and are liberally praised for doing so, they become more reflective thinkers.

The Inference and Evidence Chart (figure 6.2 and Appendix E) reflects inferences based on the following algebra problem:

> Use the digits 0, 1, 2, 3, 4, 5, 6, 7, 8, and 9 to make the equation below true. A letter must always represent the same digit. (There is more than one correct answer to this problem.)

$$
\begin{array}{r}
M\,A\,T \\
+\ \ C\,A\,T \\
\hline
B\,O\,B
\end{array}
$$

Fig. 6.2. Inference and Evidence Chart

Inference	Evidence
The digit in the ones place of each of the addends will be the same.	There is a *T* in the ones place; each letter only represents one digit.
The sum will have the same digit in the hundreds place and in the ones place.	The letter *B* is in two places; each letter represents only one digit.
The sum is less than 1,000.	There are only three letters in the sum and each one represents just one digit. So the sum has only three digits. It cannot be 1,000 or more.
The greatest number the sum could possibly be is 989.	Since we know the sum is less than 1,000 and we know that the same digit (9) is in the hundreds and ones place, the largest digit possible in the tens place is 8.
The sum of the digits in the hundreds place is less than 10.	There is no letter in the thousands place, so when *M* and *C* are added, the sum must be less than 10.
B minus *T* equals *T*.	Addition and subtraction are inverse operations. Since the problem says *T* plus *T* equals *B*, then *B* minus *T* must equal *T*.

(Adapted from Bamberger, Oberdorf, and Shultz-Farrell 2010; McGregor 2007)

Math Stretches to Encourage Students to Infer and Predict

In many Math Stretches, students may make inferences or predictions as they add a response to the chart. With the *What's the Question? Stretch*, the expectation that students will employ this strategy is made explicit.

What's the Question? Stretch

This concept was described in an earlier chapter, but it is also valuable when teaching about inferences. Because students are required to provide questions rather than answers, they must take note of the facts of the problems as well as their own prior knowledge to generate appropriate questions—in other words, they must infer what kinds of questions can be answered.

During the Math Huddle discussion spawned by this activity, students are expected to not only provide a reasonable question, but also explain what information from the problem is needed to answer it. To think of questions to add to the chart, they first identified facts from the story. Once they identified the facts, they had to recall what they already knew about answering questions. What kinds of facts are needed to answer a given question? By tapping into that prior knowledge, students' inferences allowed them to identify questions that could be answered with the information in this particular story.

For this Math Stretch, post a chart with these directions:

> *Read the following story. Use your ability to infer to help you think of a question that is not already on the chart and that can be answered given the facts in the story. Write your question on a sticky note with your initials and add it to the chart.*

> *Mrs. Solomon just moved to a new apartment. She has boxes everywhere. Each of the two bedrooms has 10 boxes in it. The living room has another 15 boxes. The kitchen has five boxes. She would like to have the boxes unpacked within four days.*

Possible student questions include:

- How many boxes does Mrs. Solomon have altogether?

- How many boxes does she have to unpack each day to have all the boxes unpacked in four days?

- Which room(s) has (or have) the greatest number of boxes?

- What are two operations you could use to find the number of boxes in the bedrooms?

- If Mrs. Solomon decides to move the boxes from the kitchen into the living room, how many boxes will be in the living room?

- When she has unpacked eight boxes, what percentage of the boxes will have been unpacked?

- How many boxes does she have to unpack to have unpacked one-half of the boxes?

- After the first day, she had unpacked 10 percent of the boxes. How many boxes are left to unpack?

By asking students to generate questions that can be answered rather than answering one given question, students are encouraged to extend their thinking. Instead of focusing on just a single mathematical aspect as they respond to this stretch, they consider a broad array of mathematical connections. Challenging students to engage in the process of inferring with stretches like *"What's the Question?"* increases their mental agility as they work with mathematical concepts and problems.

Facts or Inferences? Stretch

Students read a story scenario. Listed on the chart below the story are statements that are either facts taken from the story or inferences based on the facts in the story. Students choose a statement and decide if it is a fact from the story or an inference that was made based on the information in the story.

Read the story and the statements on this chart. Choose a statement and decide if it is a fact or an inference. If it is a fact, label it "F" and add your initials. If it is an inference, label it "I" and add your initials.

When Molly lost her dog on Saturday, she was very sad. She made a dozen posters with her dog's picture on them and put them up around her neighborhood. Every day for a week, she called the dog shelter to see if they had found her dog. She cried so much that she used up two boxes of tissues that held 50 tissues each. Finally, after 10 days, her dog returned home. Molly was so happy that she had a party and invited three friends.

- *Molly lost her dog on Saturday.* (F)

- *She made 12 posters.* (I)

- *There were four children at the party.* (I)

- *Molly used two boxes of tissues.* (F)

- *Molly's dog came home on Tuesday.* (I)

- *Molly used 100 tissues.* (I)

- *Molly called the dog pound seven times.* (I)

- *There were 50 tissues in each box.* (F)

This stretch helps students understand the difference between a fact and an inference that they may make subconsciously. For example, some students automatically think "7" when they see the term *a week* and may consider the statement *"Every day for a week"* to mean Molly called seven times, and then list this as a fact rather than an inference. The Math Huddle discussion can help correct these misconceptions and lead students to consider additional inferences to help them better understand this scenario.

In the Context of Problem Solving

Inferring and predicting can be of great value to students as they work to solve mathematical problems. The process takes making connections a step further, allowing students to use those connections to better understand possible ways to solve problems. Students are also encouraged to observe patterns and relationships and make predictions based upon their observations.

The teacher in the following small group lesson has assigned her students a game in which, working in pairs, they roll a pair of dice 10 times and find the sum of the dots with each roll. One student gets a point if the sum is even; the other student gets a point if the sum is odd. Before the game, the students are asked if the game is fair, and they all agree it is. At the end of 10 rolls, students discuss the results.

Teacher: *Everyone has finished the game now. What did you notice?*

Seth: *I don't think it was fair! Everyone who got points if the sum was even won the game. It can't be fair.*

Teacher: *Before we began the game, I asked you all if you thought it was fair. You all agreed it was.*

Serena: *But that was before we tried it. It sounded like it was fair. Half the numbers are even; the other half are odd. It should be fair.*

Teacher: *Serena, you made an inference. You thought about what you knew about even and odd numbers and then applied it to this game. You predicted that there would be just as many rolls where the sum was even as there would be when the sum was odd.*

Angel: *But, that prediction wasn't true—at least in our games.*

Teacher: *Do you think it would be if we played more games?*

Seth: *I don't think so. There were just too many even sums. It doesn't make sense.*

Teacher: *So we have a problem to solve. Sometimes, when things don't seem to make sense, it helps to break them down and look to see if there are any patterns. Let's look at this score sheet:*

$$2 + 2 = 4 \qquad even$$

$$1 + 3 = 4 \qquad even$$

$$5 + 6 = 11 \qquad odd$$

$$5 + 5 = 10 \qquad even$$

$$3 + 2 = 5 \qquad odd$$

$$1 + 6 = 7 \qquad odd$$

$$1 + 1 = 2 \qquad even$$

$$4 + 2 = 6 \qquad even$$

$$3 + 3 = 6 \qquad even$$

$$4 + 6 = 10 \qquad even$$

In this game, there were seven even sums and three odd sums. Looking at these number sentences, is there anything that you notice that might cause there to be more even than odd sums?

Serena: *Well, when we rolled, some of the rolls were even and some were odd. But the sums didn't always match up with those rolls. Look at the second one: a 1 was rolled, another odd, then a 3. It was odd, too. But the sum was even. That's strange.*

Seth: *Serena, it's strange and it makes sense, too. Remember when we made even and odd numbers with linking cubes. Odd numbers always had one left over. If both numbers had one left over, they could go together and the number would be even.*

Lei: *That means that anytime we add two odd numbers, we are going to get an even number!*

Teacher: *You all are looking at this data just like mathematicians! You used information you already knew to make an inference—that when you made even and odd numbers using pairs of cubes, the odds always had a cube left over. You inferred that when you put the cubes for the two numbers together, there would not be a cube left over. It would be an even number. Then, Lei went on to make a prediction— that anytime two odd numbers are added, the sum will be even. Do you think that is always true? Is that a conjecture we can make?*

The discussion continued as students examined the addition of two even numbers and then the addition of an even and an odd number. Students finally understood why the sums rolled in this game are more likely to be even numbers than odd numbers. Students were inferring and predicting as they worked to solve a problem arising from the results of their game. Using that comprehension strategy, they were able to make sense of a mathematical problem that at first seemed to be nonsensical.

Using Children's Literature

Students are accustomed to finding inferential meanings when reading. During literacy instruction, students are urged to "read between the lines" to understand what the author had in mind. Thus, it is a natural transition to use literature to help students learn to make mathematical, as well as literary, inferences and predictions.

During read-alouds, all students, no matter what age, enjoy listening to humorous tales. Often, in even the most fanciful story, students can be encouraged to practice inferring. *Too Cool Cows* (Speed 1995) describes the evening of two frolicking bovines, Millie and Maude. As Millie and Maude head over the mountains on their way to the moon, they are wearing "new black button-back boots" that belong to the Huckabuck kids. Students may be asked to infer how many kids are missing their boots if the cows are wearing eight boots altogether. They must think of what knowledge they already have—each child has two boots—and then figure out how many groups of two there are in eight. Later, as the children are scampering up the mountain in their bedroom slippers as they attempt to retrieve their boots from the runaway cows, students can infer that there are "40 cold toes" since they know that each child has 10 toes (4 times 10 equals 40). From there students can make predictions as to how many boots are needed for 10 cows, 20 cows, and then figure out how many kids are missing their boots in each of those situations. Practicing making inferences in these light-hearted problems can be fun.

Math-related literature can also promote students' ability to increase mathematical understanding and extend mathematical learning across the curriculum. The book *Reading the Newspaper: Estimating with Multidigit Numbers* (McMillan 2008) takes students beyond the math exploration questions already provided in the book. In a section about business news, the book displays a sample newspaper article and accompanying graph showing the growth in the number of workers for the Good Food Company (figure 6.2). Students may be asked what inferences they can draw from the increasing number of employees. They may be asked to look closely at the graph and, assuming about the same rate of yearly growth (an inference), make a prediction for the number of workers next year.

Fig. 6.2. Children's Literature Sample

36 Chapter Snapshot

As students learn that understanding mathematics is a process of actively constructing meaning, often involving the recognition of patterns and relationships, they begin to understand how important it is to be able to predict and make inferences. Although intertwined with the comprehension strategies described in previous chapters, the ability to infer and predict allows students to draw conclusions from sometimes multiple sources of mathematical information and collections of data. This strategy allows students to call upon previously attained knowledge to make sense of newly encountered mathematical situations. It is truly a fusion of what is already known with what is new, as Keene and Zimmerman (2007) express it, "a mosaic of thought."

Review and Reflect

1. Consider your days as a student. When did you first become aware of the value of making inferences and predictions? Was it taught to you explicitly? If so, in what subject areas was it taught?

2. How would you assess the abilities of your students to infer and predict? What strategies have you employed to teach your students to effectively use these skills? Have the strategies been used successfully? What instructional ideas from this chapter will you adopt in your classroom?

Chapter 7

Determining Importance

Just ask an excellent cook the value of knowing what is important and what is not. Culinary experts enjoy adding their own unique touches to familiar recipes but they know that to maintain the basic character of a recipe, they must retain the correct proportions of certain ingredients. Increasing, reducing, adding or eliminating some ingredients, however, only changes the flavor or texture. Many novice cooks have been disappointed with their efforts because they did not know the ingredients that were important to the product. Novices quickly learn to distinguish the important ingredients.

Everyone faces similar tasks in their daily lives. No matter where people turn, they are bombarded with an abundance of images and sounds. Which are important enough to merit our attention? Some information overload we filter out subconsciously. We simply tune it out—the background noise of a television, the stops and starts of traffic outside the window, or the hum of an air conditioning unit. We react differently to what is truly important to us. But when overwhelmed by a barrage of information, it is easy to overlook important facts. This is especially true for students as they work with new concepts and apply their mathematical understanding to solve problems. Unless they learn to recognize important and useful information, they grasp at facts, no matter how irrelevant they may be to the mathematical work at hand. Students should be taught that determining importance is a comprehension strategy that is as useful in mathematics as in reading.

The Levels of Determining Importance

According to Keene and Zimmerman (2007), proficient readers make decisions about the importance of what they read at three levels:

- the word level

- the sentence level

- the idea level

These reading levels can also apply to mathematical tasks and problem solving. When engaged in mathematical communication, written or oral, proficient mathematicians make judgments about the relative importance of the words, sentences, and ideas based on their own background knowledge, the purpose for their interaction with the communication, and sometimes, even their own particular interests. Furthermore, text features, such as italics or bold print, may prompt mathematics readers to assign a greater level of importance to certain words or sentences.

Word Level

The use of precise and math-specific vocabulary is a characteristic of mathematical communication, whether it is relating a detailed examination of a mathematical concept, an explanation of a mathematical process, or a description of a problem. Students should be alert to the occurrence of these specialized mathematical terms and focus on the meaning of the sentences in which they appear. Some text features (e.g., bold print, italics, highlights) cue students to words of particular importance. Without explicit instruction about the utility of text features in mathematical reading, students may overlook their significance.

Sentence Level

Certain sentences carry more weight and are more important than others. Students should know that a sentence containing important mathematical words will probably also be one that is meaningful and worthy of attention. If students understand how to interpret text features to identify words significant to the content of the reading, they will be cued to important sentences, too.

Knowing the typical structure of mathematical word problems may also aid students as they read for meaning. Quite often, the first sentence in a word problem introduces the context of the problem, but contains little important information. Most of the important facts are found in the middle of the problem. Typically, there is a question at the end of the problem that lets students know what they are expected to find. Students should be aware of this structure, but should also know that some problems are structured differently. Instead of teaching the structure as a shortcut that eliminates the need for thinking, it should be taught as an aid that may assist in distinguishing essential information from irrelevant facts.

Idea Level

The ultimate goal for learners, of course, is determining importance at the idea level. What are the "big" mathematical ideas? What is the overall meaning of the problem scenario? Students need help to navigate their way through the details, so they can focus on the significant ideas in their mathematical work. Understanding the important words and sentences is essential to recognizing the critical mathematical ideas in reading, exploring concepts, or solving problems. Students' skills at those levels must be carefully developed to ensure that they fully understand and recognize the major concepts.

Reading mathematical text is often a particular challenge to students. They tend to be more successful picking out critical ideas when reading fictional narratives which are more familiar in content and format. Provide more support and scaffolding for students when they read texts with less familiar content and formats.

Critically Examining Mathematical Information

Beyond identifying what is crucial to understanding, mathematicians have to read critically—"with a healthy dose of skepticism" (Keene and Zimmermann 2007). Readers of mathematics often grapple with numeric information. Students need to understand that data may be manipulated by authors to portray a "certain version of reality" (Whitin and Whitin 2011). Whitin and Whitin argue that "mathematical information is human construct, and not a sacrosanct edifice of unassailable truths." The ability to critically evaluate both mathematical literature and numerical information to discern its validity and credibility is a prerequisite for capturing its essence.

What Students Need to Know about Determining Importance

Proficient mathematicians recognize the need to determine the relative importance of the mathematical information with which they work. Just as with reading (Keene and Zimmerman 2007; Harvey and Goudvis 2007), students need to know that:

1. Mathematicians make decisions, both intentionally and spontaneously, about what is important in mathematical communication at the word, sentence, and idea level.

2. Mathematicians make decisions about importance based on:

    - mathematical purpose (e.g., exploring and understanding mathematical concepts, solving problems, interpreting data, sharing ideas)

    - background knowledge

    - knowledge of text features and structures

    - ideas shared during related mathematical discussions with others

3. Mathematicians can explain how they decide what is important and how using this strategy enhances their mathematical understanding.

4. Mathematicians critically evaluate the validity of mathematical text and numeric information as they determine its importance.

5. Mathematicians use the information they identify as important to help them reason mathematically, justify mathematical thinking, understand mathematical concepts, and to solve problems.

Mathematicians make decisions, both intentionally and spontaneously, about what is important in mathematical communication at the word, sentence, and idea level.

Mathematicians, as they interact with the communication of mathematical ideas or numerical data, are constantly "sorting and sifting" (Harvey and Goudvis 2007) to identify the most important and relevant aspects of information. This is often a spontaneous, almost subconscious, process. With experience, proficient mathematicians deftly recognize the need-to-know facts allowing them to strategically read with their mathematical needs in mind.

When it does not occur spontaneously, determining importance is a comprehension strategy that may be intentionally applied to increase understanding. Help students to deliberately pick out the most relevant and important points in their math-related communications at all levels (word, sentence, and idea) as a way of increasing their comprehension of a given concept or problem. Students must realize that this is a skill that can be honed through practice and eventually leads to a more automatic, spontaneous application of this comprehension strategy.

Mathematicians make decisions about importance based on:

- mathematical purpose (e.g., exploring and understanding mathematical concepts, solving problems, interpreting data, sharing ideas)

- background knowledge

- knowledge of text features and structures

- ideas shared during related mathematical discussions with others

The goals and purposes of mathematicians influence their decisions about what is important. When students read textbooks to help them understand a new concept, any information that clarifies the concept is important (Owocki 2003). When students are engaged in applying their mathematical knowledge to solve problems, reading and understanding the problem is a critical step. The determination of what is important is germane to solving problems.

A mathematician's prior knowledge impacts how he or she determines importance. If an understanding of a concept already exists, explanatory information may not be important. Without that understanding, however, explanatory information is vital.

Experienced mathematicians, like proficient readers, take advantage of what they know about text features and text structures. Text features offer readers explicit cues to help them distinguish essential information from details of less importance (Harvey and Goudvis 2007). Words emphasized with bold fonts or italics may be significant. Illustrations, photographs, and diagrams may contain information essential to understanding. Headings and subheadings may point readers to specific sections of the mathematical text containing valuable information. Additionally, knowing the typical structure of word problems may facilitate locating facts necessary for comprehending and solving problems.

Finally, mathematicians make decisions about the relative importance of ideas based on thoughts shared by others during collaborative work or discussions. Verbal exchanges often lead to new questions and areas of inquiry—and as a consequence, additional information may be considered relevant and important.

Mathematicians can explain how they decide what is important and how using this strategy enhances their mathematical understanding.

Young mathematicians should learn the value of premeditation the process of determining importance. It is unrealistic to expect that the use of this strategy just comes naturally. They need to know that, with practice, they will become more proficient and its use will become spontaneous.

Model and think aloud to demonstrate how to determine what is important in mathematical materials and resources. Explicitly describe your thinking as you choose the important words, sentences, and ideas to help students envision how the strategy is applied. Furthermore, explain how determining the relative importance of the mathematical information increases your understanding. Include both *how* to use the strategy and *why* it is beneficial.

Mathematicians critically evaluate the validity of mathematical text and numeric information as they determine its importance.

The importance of mathematical ideas and data may depend on validity. To be mathematically literate, we must be competent at assessing the validity of the mathematical text and numerical information we encounter in real-life situations. Students should develop a healthy skepticism of the mathematical ideas and data with which they work and "probe beneath the surface to uncover the assumptions, expose motives, and raise issues about power and control" (Whitin and Whitin 2011). In critically examining mathematical materials, all modes of expression should be considered. In text, word choice and the assumed definitions of terms may impact meaning. Astute mathematicians know that the method of collecting the data, and even the visual elements of the data, affect meaning.

Support students as they develop the capacity to evaluate the integrity of mathematical information by thinking-aloud as you analyze mathematical data.. Frequent opportunities to collect and represent data in multiple ways allow students to become familiar with the process and to develop their understanding of how the process may be manipulated. In addition, students develop a critical eye by having ample chances to discuss, examine, and interpret data with others.

Mathematicians use the information they identify as important to help them reason mathematically, justify mathematical thinking, understand mathematical concepts, and to solve problems.

It may seem obvious that once the important ideas are identified, they can be used to reason, justify thinking, understand concepts, and solve problems. But students need to be explicitly taught that there is indeed a purpose for this strategy other than just the application of the strategy. It is easy to lose sight of the fact that the end goal of the use of comprehension strategies is increased understanding. As teachers began using these strategies during literacy instruction, mastery of the strategy sometimes became more important than comprehending the reading. If too much time is focused on practicing a strategy to the exclusion of actually employing it in a worthwhile way to make meaning, its value is diminished.

Mathematicians base their reasoning on the mathematical ideas that they have determined to be important. They call on these ideas as they justify their own thinking. They reflect on them as they work to understand new concepts. They draw upon them as they solve mathematical problems. Students need encouragement and opportunities to do the same.

Teasing the Important Ideas from Mathematical Text

Students must focus on important information and merge it with their background knowledge to construct new meaning or solve problems. This process is more effective when facts and details are linked to larger concepts or big ideas. As students sift through the facts and details in mathematical text, the big ideas are very easily obscured by minutiae. Only by separating the significant from the mundane will the big ideas become more apparent. Once the big ideas are identified, the facts and details tend to fall into place and are more readily understood.

The challenge is teaching students how to discern the significant information, to tease it out from the overall text. As Harvey and Goudvis (2007) lamented, "This is easier said than done." Even after years of schooling, many college students highlight sentence after sentence in their assigned texts as they try to identify the most important facts. Later, as they review what they read, the pages are awash in a sea of yellow or pink or blue. These students are frustrated and struggle to locate the most important concepts in their reading.

Provide instruction beginning in the primary grades on how to sort the essential information from the irrelevant. With ongoing and consistent instruction, students can learn to read carefully and critically—identifying the most important ideas.

Overviewing

Particularly effective for accessing the meaning of expository writing is overviewing (Harvey and Goudvis 2007). Students learn to skim textual materials before reading to locate areas of important words, sentences, and ideas. Students need explicit instruction and modeling in this skill to appreciate the thinking and analysis requirements.

Practice overviewing during shared reading. Using a large display of the text, explain your thought process as you choose and label the parts of the text that are most important. Students should be able to see the labeled parts of the text.

To further support students as they practice overviewing, provide mini-lessons on:

- finding the purpose for reading

- activating background knowledge to make mathematical connections

- knowing which text features may aid in the location of critical information

- recognizing when to pay careful attention to the text

- determining what may be ignored without detracting from the meaning

- discovering the relationship of facts and details to the big idea

- assessing the value of the text relative to the purpose for reading (if it contains no relevant information or if it requires careful reading)

The overview process also serves as a preview prior to reading. It gives students an idea of what to expect as they read. As a result of the overview, they begin to reflect on their current understanding of the mathematics, make predictions that can be proved or disproved, and create a visual outline of the structure of the text.

In addition, when students are reading word problems, it is almost impossible for them to identify what parts of the text are important until they read the final question. Since that crucial information is most often at the end of the problem, overviewing encourages students to first skim through to the end where they can locate that information. When they return to the text, they can read more thoroughly with the final question in mind.

Highlighting

Highlighting only works when the person highlighting is actively considering the parts of the text that merit a highlight. Too much highlighting simply obscures the distinction between relevant and irrelevant sections of the text.

Harvey and Goudvis (2007) recommend having students note the reasons for the highlight on a sticky note near the highlighted text. These notes require students to assess the value of the information in regard to the purpose for reading. Certainly, with considerable amounts of reading, this would be cumbersome. For the amount of mathematical reading that most students do, however, the task is manageable and reinforces the purpose of highlighting.

Sometimes students have trouble distinguishing truly important ideas from facts that are interesting to them (Harvey and Goudvis 2007). Teachers need to recognize that students may reasonably impart importance to details that make an impression on them whether or not they lead to understanding the mathematics at hand.

While acknowledging the legitimacy of determining points important to an individual, help students separate facts and details of purely personal importance from those that are crucial for making mathematical meaning. Modeling this thought process provides chances for students to discuss their own thoughts as they make these distinctions.

As part of the modeling process, give students two different colors— one color to highlight the mathematically important ideas and the other to mark ideas of personal importance. Students should be cautioned that their focus on the mathematical issues must be foremost—highlighting of solely individual points of interest should be very limited.

To highlight skillfully, practice is necessary. Students need opportunities for guided practice. Encourage them to share their reasons for highlighting specific areas of the text with partners, in a small group, or with the whole class, thus expanding the range of student thinking about what is and is not important in a text and holding them accountable.

Read a Little, Think a Little

Murphy (2010) suggests a technique called Read a Little, Think a Little to support students as they practice determining importance. With this approach, the text is divided into smaller, more manageable bites, so the task is not quite so daunting.

Upon reading each chunk, students pause to assimilate what they have read and to identify its most salient ideas. Students are encouraged to not just "read" the words in each chunk of text, but to really consider their meaning, asking themselves: What did I just read? What was the essence of what I just read?

Natural text breaks such as paragraphs may serve to divide the text by highlighting, using sticky notes, or recording the facts on a teacher-developed form. When reading short word problems, however, it may be more effective to break the text down into individual sentences. Indicate the relevant and important information from each chunk, use sticky notes, or record facts on a teacher-developed form. Although highlighting pertinent sections of the text is widely used and may be an efficient way to indicate important information, having students record the ideas in their own words may be a more beneficial method. Reading research shows that when students translate what they have read into their own words, they are able to more easily retrieve those ideas and apply them (Brummer and Macceca 2008).

Before students are expected to independently apply the Read a Little, Think a Little approach, they must be taught how to do it. Begin with teacher modeling, next guided practice, and finally independent practice with specific ongoing feedback. The Read a Little, Think a Little method of analyzing text supplies scaffolding as students build proficiency at determining importance. As with any form of scaffolding, teachers should consider when and how to gradually withdraw that scaffolding so that students develop the capacity to recognize relevant and important ideas as they read mathematical materials without the imposition of a supporting structure.

Teaching Students to Determine Mathematical Importance

Traditionally, understanding and interpreting mathematical text was considered to be the realm of mathematics teachers. This type of text is, in many ways, much more abstract and demanding of a reader than fiction or even most nonfiction. If students failed to develop the ability to construct meaning from its content, concern about this deficiency was limited.

That is changing, however, with emergence of the digital age. Quantification and data analysis are entering the realm of language, history, and the arts with the advent of the digital humanities (Cohen 2010). In all disciplines, the ability to read mathematical texts and interpret numerical information is now essential.

As never before, it is incumbent on teachers to give students the support that they need to develop the capacity to read and interpret mathematical materials with agility and understanding. Teaching students to use comprehension strategies, described by Hyde (2006) as "vehicles to help us find our way through the maze of possibilities," effectively boosts understanding when applied to this genre. Of the comprehension strategies, determining importance is certainly one of the most valuable when reading mathematical resources.

Modeling and Think-Alouds

One of the most constructive elements to model for students as they examine text for important ideas is the value of slowing down and reflecting. Students often mistakenly equate speed with ability. They are hesitant to pause and reflect in case they appear incapable of reading quickly. Some students also just want to complete the task. Their goal is simply hurrying to finish rather than understanding the mathematics at its core. Model the process of pausing to reflect and assess the relative importance of what has been read. Think aloud to help students realize that reading with reflection and understanding is better than reading quickly. Impress on students that identifying the relevant and important parts of the text represents successful completion of the task—that mathematical reading, like any other reading, is more than just naming each word.

Below, a teacher models how to determine importance with the book, *Collecting Data* (McMillan 2008). Copies of the pages are enlarged and displayed so students can read along. The teacher wants to model pausing to reflect and examine text features that may point to important information.

> **Teacher:** *I've found a great book about data. We have been talking about how we can better understand what we read if we focus on information that is important. Before I begin, I know that information related to data is going to be of special interest to me. There is so much in this book I can't possibly remember it all, so I am going to decide what's most important.*

The teacher shows students the title page and table of contents and begins the think-aloud on the page, shown below.

Teacher: *I'm going to read the first page slowly, so I can really focus on it.*

The teacher reads aloud.

Teacher: *This page tells me a lot! I noticed that some words are in bold print. That tells me I should pay attention to those. They might even be in the glossary. The first word is* data. *Right after the word, the text tells me it means "information." Let me write that down on my chart.*

The teacher records *data means information* on a chart labeled "Important Information about Data."

Teacher: *Next I see the words* **scientists** *and* **community**. *Those are people who collect data. I'm not sure how important those words are to me right now. I'm going to keep them in mind because they are in bold print, but I know I have to really focus on the most important facts about data.*

At the bottom of the page, I see a green box. I bet the information in that box is important, too. It tells me again that data is another word for "information." And, **research** *is another word in bold print. I think that may be important. I'm going to add to the chart that "people use data they collect for research." That's not exactly the way the book said it, but I want to use my own words because that helps me understand it.*

So far, the teacher has deliberately led students to consider the text features on this page that may help them focus on significant information. The think-aloud has also shown students how it is not always clear as one reads what is the most important information. The teacher turns to the next page (see page 213) and reads it.

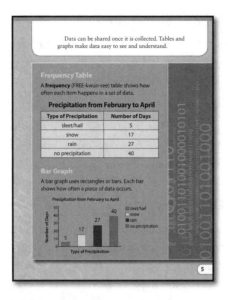

Data can be shared once it is collected. Tables and graphs make data easy to see and understand.

Frequency Table

A **frequency** (FREE-kwun-see) table shows how often each item happens in a set of data.

Precipitation from February to April

Type of Precipitation	Number of Days
sleet/hail	5
snow	17
rain	27
no precipitation	40

Bar Graph

A bar graph uses rectangles or bars. Each bar shows how often a piece of data occurs.

5

Teacher: *On this page, I see text, but I also see a table and a graph. I need to pay close attention to them. From the text at the top of the page, I learned that tables and graphs make data easy to see and understand. I think that is important. I'm adding it to my chart.*

Now looking at the green box, I see frequency table *is in bold print. I think I need to know what a frequency table is. It shows how often something happens. I'm adding that to my chart. I already know what a bar graph is, so I don't need to add that. And, I don't think I need to remember all the data in the table or the graph. Maybe if I was reading to find out more about weather, that would be important to me, but I'm not.*

Sometimes when I read something the first time, I just hurry through it. But it really helps me pick out important information if I slow down and think about what I read, bit by bit. The bold print and green boxes point out things that might be important for me to remember, too. Even so, I always have to think it through myself. I can't just assume something is important because it is in bold print. I might already know it or it might not really be important for my purposes.

Whenever you read about mathematics, be sure to slow down and think about what parts are most important. When you do that, you will understand not only more about what you are reading, but more about mathematics.

Following a think-aloud, specify exactly what you were trying to model so that it is very clear to students. Or, ask students what they noticed about the process. After students share their observations, explain any aspects of the modeling that students failed to notice.

Building on the Concrete

For younger students, it is difficult to understand the abstract concept of sorting information of importance from other facts and details that may be equally as interesting. If you connect an abstract idea to something more concrete, it is more likely to be grasped by students of all ages. McGregor (2007) suggests the following demonstrations to help students remember what determining importance is all about:

To begin this demonstration, the teacher reminds students how difficult it is for our brains to remember everything we read and that thoughtful readers use a strategy—determining importance—that allows them to pick out the important ideas and cast away the things that don't matter. Students are asked to watch a demonstration of what a reader's brain does as it uses this strategy. They are reminded to always think of "how two pans, a strainer, and some spaghetti can represent determining importance when you read."

The teacher places the strainer atop an empty pan and proceeds to slowly pour a pot of water and spaghetti through the strainer. As the dripping strainer is lifted from the pan that now contains the water, students are told that this is about what our brains do when they are determining importance. Rather than explain the connection, the teacher encourages communication by asking students to turn to a partner and make sense of what they have just seen. Once students have shared their ideas with a partner, the whole class comes together to share their ideas as the teacher facilitates the discussion. The teacher ensures that students understand that the important facts, or spaghetti, have been separated out from the unimportant, or the water, just as learners have to tease out the important ideas when reading or working with mathematics. Without a doubt, students won't forget the visual images of this demonstration and will forever connect it with determining importance.

What's Important?

What is important in reading always depends on the purpose for reading. To demonstrate how to link purpose to the process of determining importance, teachers may present a story problem with plenty of facts, but no questions. With virtually no criteria for determining importance, students quickly discover that every fact in the problem has to be considered important. They have no basis on which to filter the information in the story. The purpose for reading the story problem is missing since there is no answer to find.

Once this idea has been established and discussed, the teacher may provide several questions that can be answered from the facts in the story scenario, each recorded on a sheet of chart paper. Students are divided into groups. Each group is assigned one of the questions and asked to identify what information is important for that particular question. When the groups have completed their work, they come together in a Math Huddle to consider what they have learned. As they examine the charts and the important facts for each question, students see how the purpose for reading affects what is deemed important. The exercise makes it obvious how vital it is to have a purpose in reading and then to identify importance relative to that purpose.

Zoom In/Zoom Out

One of the reasons students are assigned word problems is to connect abstract mathematical concepts with real-life applications, but for many students, understanding the problem itself is as difficult as understanding the mathematical concepts used to solve it. They struggle with figuring out what is happening in the stated problem, in addition to comprehending what information is essential to solving the problem and whether any additional information is needed.

After using the "zooming" features on some websites, Thompson created a process called Zoom In/Zoom Out (Thompson et al. 2008) and applied it to problem solving. This task encourages students to examine the details of a problem as they zoom in, and then zoom out to gain a more holistic view that puts the details of the problem in perspective.

To use Zoom In/Zoom Out, first have students read and make sense of the problem. Next, as they collaborate with a peer, have them share their thoughts on the problem, what they are asked to find, the details of the problem, and identification of any additional information they need. The collaborative effort encourages students to compare and revise their interpretations of the problem, if desired.

Next, bring the class together to "zoom in" and closely examine the information from the problem—clarifying the meaning of any unfamiliar vocabulary and math-related symbols or expressions. During this segment of this task, students scrutinize the facts of the problem and determine which are crucial to solving it. Students self-assess their initial interpretations and work with their peers in light of the ideas shared by the whole class.

Then, lead the class to "zoom out" and focus on the more holistic aspect of the problem, its overall objective, as they also consider possible solution methods. In the final step of Zoom In/Zoom Out, students assume the responsibility of solving the problem independently. Then, they share their strategies orally with their peers and write about their problem-solving processes.

Zoom In/Zoom Out provides opportunities for students to work in several ways—independently, collaboratively with peers, and as part of the whole class—as they examine mathematical problems. This approach helps students become proficient at determining importance. As they examine the problem independently and then collaborate with a peer, they begin to identify crucial information.

The process continues as the class "zooms in" on the problem and additional opinions are shared about the significance of the facts. Then, as the focus shifts with the "zoom out" phase, students are able to check to see whether they correctly identified the essential information that they needed to understand and solve the problem.

Math Stretches to Support Determining Importance

The *What's Most Important about _____? Stretch* helps students develop an understanding of what "determining importance" means and the ability to sort through information, weighing its value relative to other pieces of information, and choosing what they think is most important about a mathematical concept or topic. Once students have selected what they think is most important, they must also justify their choices in mathematical terms.

Post a chart labeled, *"What's Most Important about _____?"* (figure 7.1). Students are directed to reflect on the mathematical area that you fill in. For example, you may decide to address the order of operations. As students add what they believe to be the most important aspect of the order of operations, they must also add a written justification for their choice, drawing upon their mathematical knowledge. When all students have responded, call students to a Math Huddle to discuss their thinking.

Fig. 7.1. Sample What's Most Important about the Order of Operations? Chart

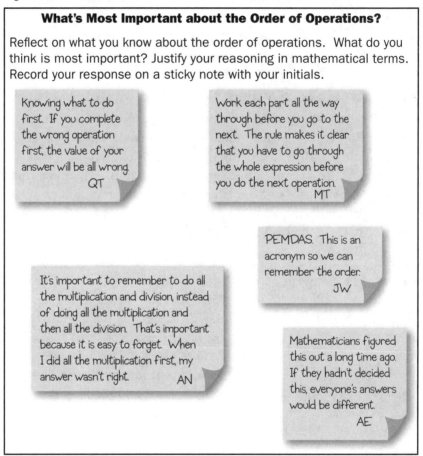

What's Most Important about the Order of Operations?

Reflect on what you know about the order of operations. What do you think is most important? Justify your reasoning in mathematical terms. Record your response on a sticky note with your initials.

Knowing what to do first. If you complete the wrong operation first, the value of your answer will be all wrong.
QT

Work each part all the way through before you go to the next. The rule makes it clear that you have to go through the whole expression before you do the next operation.
MT

PEMDAS. This is an acronym so we can remember the order.
JW

It's important to remember to do all the multiplication and division, instead of doing all the multiplication and then all the division. That's important because it is easy to forget. When I did all the multiplication first, my answer wasn't right.
AN

Mathematicians figured this out a long time ago. If they hadn't decided this, everyone's answers would be different.
AE

As students contribute and justify their ideas as to what they think is most significant about the order of operations, the teacher is able to gain insight into the way they approach the task of determining importance as well as assess their mathematical understanding of the concept.

In figure 7.1 (above) a misconception was posted on the chart. One student expressed the belief that an operation is carried throughout the expression before going on to the next, rather than understanding that multiplication and division are completed together, followed by addition and subtraction. The teacher can correct this misconception with the entire class during the Math Huddle. The teacher may also choose to discuss it further with this student in a one-on-one conference or convene a small group session to revisit order of operations.

Students benefit from the practice of applying this comprehension strategy, reflecting on what they have learned, preparing a mathematical justification for their thinking, and from sharing the thoughts of other students as they participate in the discourse.

In the Context of Problem Solving

Surprisingly, the NCTM (2000) standards and the accompanying overview focus very little on the ability to understand a problem. The problem-solving standard states that students should be able to:

- build new mathematical knowledge through problem solving

- solve problems that arise in mathematics and in other contexts

- apply and adapt a variety of appropriate strategies to solve problems

- monitor and reflect on the process of mathematical problem solving

It may be argued that understanding the problem is a prerequisite for solving a problem. Even in the overview, however, the only reference to understanding problems is, "Effective problem solvers constantly monitor and adjust what they are doing. They make sure they understand the problem. If a problem is written down, they read it carefully; if it is told to them orally, they ask questions until they understand." The overview text then moves on to the importance of planning how to solve a problem. Little guidance is given on how to help students understand a problem.

The newly developed Common Core State Standards (2009) address the issue of understanding a little more directly in the Standards for Mathematical Practice stating, "Mathematically proficient students start by explaining to themselves the meaning of a problem and looking for entry points to its solutions. They analyze givens, constraints, relationships and goals." But, even with these standards, no guidance is provided as to how to help students develop the ability to comprehend the problem.

In spite of the early work of Pólya, whose first step in problem solving was "understand the problem," little attention has been brought to bear on what instructional strategies are most effective in helping students develop the skills they need to fully understand word problems. With the demands of increasingly rigorous standards that require students to be able to apply the mathematical concepts they are learning to solve contextual problems, this is an area of concern for many teachers.

Foremost in solving problems is the identification of the important facts in the problem. Teaching students how to determine importance fosters their ability to understand and focus on the essential facts of the problem.

Some consider word problems a genre in and of themselves, thoroughly embedded within the mathematics curriculum (Gerofsky 2004).

Understanding their structure aids students in their efforts to identify the important information in a problem. Gerofsky describes the typical three-part structure as follows:

- **The set-up component:** the setting, context, situation, and characters are introduced

- **The information component:** the important information for solving the problem is provided as well as some nonessential and even irrelevant facts

- **The question component:** informs the problem solver of the question to be answered

Awareness of a typical story problem structure is an asset in determining importance. Knowing where to most likely find the important facts enhances the ability of students to find them. Given the textual structure outlined by Gerofsky, students can be taught where to begin looking for the information they need to solve a problem.

In general, the set-up component contains little information pertinent to the solution of the problem. Students are advised to look to the middle section of a problem where the relevant facts are most commonly given. They must still carefully consider any factual information within this section because some of it may be irrelevant to the problem. Finally, students should know to look to the end of the problem to determine what it is they must find to solve the problem.

During the first reading of a problem, students are rarely able to reliably determine importance because they do not yet know what they are expected to find out. Until they have read the problem through and understand the question, attempts to do so are futile. Encourage students to routinely read problems at least twice. With the second reading, the question is understood, so the process of determining which facts are relevant and which are not can be accomplished.

As with following any general guidelines, students must always carefully consider the entire problem. Not all problems are constructed according to the typical word problem structure. Students know that they have to think carefully as they consider what is vital and relevant to solving any problem, but knowing the general story problem format may make it easier to determine the important information.

Using Children's Literature

Many students have practiced determining importance to help them understand literature. Use children's literature as a transitional starting point for teaching them to apply this strategy to mathematical reading. During read-alouds, pose problems based on the details of the story. Together, the class can determine what information from the story is important in solving the problem.

One example of this is the use of the popular story, *Caps for Sale* by Esphyr Slobodkina (1940). On the first page of this tale, the reader learns that a peddler carries his caps on top of his head. In addition to his own checked cap, he has gray caps, brown caps, blue caps, and red caps. Accompanying the text is an illustration of the peddler with the stack of caps upon his head. After reading this page and showing students the illustration, the following dialogue might occur:

Teacher: *Can you imagine carrying all those hats on your head? I wonder how many caps he had altogether. Can you think of how we might find out?*

Mason: *We could look at the picture and count them.*

Teacher: *That is one way we could do it. There are a lot of caps to count. Can anyone think of another way?*

Sondra: *We know how many different color hats he has. It looks like he has the same number of each color. Maybe we could count by that number—like when we skip count.*

Teacher: *Let's stop and think about Sondra's idea for a minute. What information do we have to have to use her problem-solving approach?*

Lee: *We have to know how many different color hats the seller has.*

Teacher: *Does the text tell us that?*

Lee: *Yes. He has a checked hat, then gray, brown, blue, and red. So—five in all!*

Sondra: *But we know he only has one checked hat.*

Teacher: *Why is that important to know, Sondra?*

Sondra: *For all the other colors, he has the same number—four each. I can tell by the picture. If you are going to skip count, there have to be the same number in each group.*

Mason: *So if we count by four—we have four gray. Then, with the brown, we have eight. The blue brings it to 12.*

Sondra: *With the red—we have 16 caps!*

Mason: *Don't forget the one he was wearing. Altogether, that is 17.*

Teacher: *So, to solve this problem, we had to find some important information from the story. We had to know how many different colors of caps the peddler has and how many caps of each color. Did the story give us the information we needed?*

Lee: *Not all of it. It told us the colors.*

Mason: *To find the rest, we used the picture.*

Teacher: *We just used a valuable strategy to help us understand the problem so we could solve it. We had to determine what information from the story was important. Once you thought of a way we could solve it, you went back to the story and picked out the really important information. That is one strategy that mathematicians use to understand mathematical ideas and problems. Remember that strategy whenever you are working like a mathematician.*

Math-related literature may also be used to provide students practice in determining importance. Greg Tang's book, *The Grapes of Math: Mind-Stretching Math Riddles* (2001) presents readers with math riddles that encourage students to think creatively and efficiently during the problem-solving process. Although the book does not address determining importance, it provides an excellent vehicle for practicing this strategy. Each riddle can be solved in a variety of ways. As students suggest solutions, they can also be challenged to identify the important information needed to solve the riddles.

Integrating children's literature into mathematics instruction motivates students as they explore mathematics concepts in their literary context. In addition, students recognize the universal role of the comprehension strategies—making meaning when reading, making meaning when exploring mathematics.

Chapter Snapshot

Paramount to understanding mathematical ideas or problems is recognizing what is important. What are the key ideas of a math concept? What are the essential facts needed to solve a problem? Because students are so deluged with information and sensory stimulation, some tend to tune out everything unless it captures their immediate attention.

Through classroom experiences that help students learn to intentionally and with purpose examine and filter incoming information, they can become more proficient at recognizing and retaining the information that is important for comprehension of mathematical concepts or problems. When students clearly identify their purpose for reading mathematical materials, they can more readily distinguish between relevant and irrelevant facts. When students learn and then apply what they know about text features and text structures, these tasks become easier for them. As students become more capable of sorting information according to its importance, they also become more critical readers and mathematical thinkers.

Review and Reflect

1. Consider a real-life problem you have had to solve. How did you identify important information that you needed to solve it? How can you apply your own experience to the instructional goal of helping students distinguish essential information from irrelevant facts as they explore mathematical ideas or solve problems?

2. What ideas from this chapter do you plan to use in your classroom? Why did you choose those specific ideas? How might you adapt them?

3. Although students must develop a deep conceptual understanding of mathematical concepts, the success of many teachers is measured by their students' performance on standardized tests. In these high-stakes tests, students encounter a variety of word problems. In what ways can teachers help students to determine importance during mathematics tests?

Chapter 8

Synthesizing Information

Mathematics is a science of ideas and processes that have a pattern of regularity and order (Van de Walle, Karp, and Bay-Williams 2010). Making sense of these often complex relationships and patterns is at the very heart of the discipline. Blending disparate pieces of information with prior knowledge, mathematicians, like proficient readers, construct new understanding.

Mathematicians are forever engaged in the process of "ordering, combining, and recreating into a coherent whole the mass of information that bombards our minds every day" (Keene and Zimmermann 2007). Similar to the ripples caused by throwing a rock into a pool of water, meaning expands, and according to Miller (2002), "simple elements of thought [are] transformed into a complex whole."

Keene and Zimmermann (1997) compare synthesis, the process of sifting through a multitude of details, focusing on the most relevant and then organizing those ideas, to the meticulous creation of a "mosaic of meaning, a beauty, greater than the sum of each shiny piece." Synthesizing takes place during and after reading, and the results are continually revised as new information is encountered or recalled. At its most meaningful, new and existing information is merged to generate an entirely new and original idea, a new perspective, or a new line of thinking (Harvey and Goudvis 2000).

The process of synthesizing information may be the most complex of the comprehension strategies. It builds on the successful implementation of the other strategies, as needed for understanding. It requires "fusing our learning, unlearning, and relearning. It's about valuing the process of our thinking, becoming reflective thinkers, remembering where we come from and where we're going" (McGregor 2007).

Strands of Mathematical Proficiency

The authors of *Adding It Up: Helping Children Learn Mathematics* (National Research Council 2001) describe five intertwined strands or components of mathematical proficiency:

- Conceptual understanding

- Procedural fluency

- Strategic competence

- Productive disposition

- Adaptive reasoning

Together these strands represent a complex whole—interwoven and interdependent. All are necessary for the development of mathematical proficiency. The interwoven nature of these strands reflects their finding that "a deep understanding requires that learners connect pieces of knowledge, and that connection in turn is a key factor in whether they can use what they know productively in solving problems" (National Research Council 2001). In other words, learners of mathematics must be able to synthesize.

Within these interwoven strands, the *conceptual understanding* strand requires that learners have an integrated and functional grasp of mathematical ideas—the kind of understanding that supports retention. *Procedural fluency* refers to the knowledge of procedures— when and how they are used as well as proficiency in using them "flexibly, accurately, and efficiently." To be *strategically competent*, students must be capable of formulating, representing, and solving mathematical problems. Learners demonstrate a *productive disposition* when they see that mathematics makes sense and is useful. If they believe that effort pays off, they view themselves as effective learners and doers of mathematics. And, finally, *adaptive reasoning* is defined as the ability to reflect logically about relationships among concepts and situations. Adaptive reasoning is another way of referring to the analytic thinking processes of synthesis.

The concept of adaptive reasoning goes beyond the notions of formal proof and deductive reasoning to include informal explanations and justifications, as well as "intuitive and inductive reasoning based on pattern, analogy, and metaphor" (English 2004). The use of analogy, the ability to reason with relational patterns, is essential for students as they develop the capacity to synthesize. With synthesis, the previous knowledge of students serves as a basis for the generation of new knowledge and for solving unfamiliar problems (National Research Council 2001). The ability to synthesize, therefore, not only enables students to comprehend mathematical ideas, but also forms the foundation for one of the strands that comprise mathematical proficiency.

Synthesizing and Mathematizing

Synthesis is also integral to Fosnot's and Dolk's notion of mathematizing. They state that mathematizing is what mathematicians do as they actively construct meaning by "setting up quantifiable and spatial relationships, by noticing patterns and transformations, by proving them as generalizations, and by searching for elegant solutions" (2001). Creativity in recognizing relationships and generalizations, then synthesizing them with existing mathematical knowledge, is at its core. In essence, synthesis is the catalyst for the construction of mathematical meaning.

Because mathematical learning is complex, students need ample opportunities to dynamically interact with strategies, big ideas, and models as they struggle to make sense of real-life, challenging mathematical experiences. Genuine mathematizing involves "searching for patterns, constructing models, and proposing conjectures and proving them" (Fosnot and Dolk 2001). Through these interactions, students should be encouraged to see, organize, and interpret the world through a mathematical lens.

To make sense of their mathematical experiences, students interpret, organize, and establish models based on the foundation of ideas and strategies they have already acquired. New mathematical meaning is built on the foundations of existing ideas; existing ideas are reformulated based on newly discovered information. By exploring mathematical issues and examining new ideas in the context of existing schema, students become proficient at synthesizing their mathematical experiences, and they actively "mathematize."

The mathematical activity of students is what distinguishes mathematizing from the traditional teacher-delivered approach of teaching mathematics. According to Fosnot and Dolk (2001), "Children, in learning to mathematize their world, will come to see mathematics as the living discipline it is, with themselves a part of a creative, constructive mathematical community, hard at work."

What Students Need to Know about Synthesizing

Synthesis is inherent in the work of mathematicians as it is in reading for comprehension (Keene and Zimmerman 2007). Students need to understand that:

1. Mathematicians are aware of changes in mathematical thinking through additional mathematical experiences.

2. Mathematicians synthesize ideas when they consider their new mathematical experiences in light of the existing mathematical knowledge to construct new mathematical meaning.

3. Mathematicians understand that a synthesis is the sum of information from new mathematical experiences and existing mathematical knowledge that leads to new ideas or understanding.

4. Mathematicians know their knowledge of math continues to evolve as new information or ideas are encountered.

5. Mathematicians can explain how using synthesis helps them to better understand mathematics.

Mathematicians are aware of changes in their mathematical thinking through additional mathematical experiences.

Mathematical knowledge is rarely static. Students consciously think about new mathematical experiences as they engage in them and assimilate the new information through the process of synthesis.

Reflection is crucial to building new understanding. Students should consciously examine their thinking and understanding as they encounter new mathematical materials or experiences: *What new ideas am I encountering? Do the new ideas align with what I already know? Do I need to adjust my thinking?* As students turn ideas over in their heads, consider the experiences from different points of view, and step back to examine the experiences anew, their reflections help them recognize new relationships and increase understanding (Hiebert et al. 1997).

Mathematicians synthesize ideas when they consider their new mathematical experiences in light of existing knowledge to construct new mathematical meaning.

Students should check their new ideas for consistency with their previous ideas: *If thinking does not align, is there faulty data? Is there a new concept emerging that is based on a different set of parameters? What existing information or ideas do I have that might justify these new relationships and patterns? How can I merge the new information with what I already know?* Thus, in essence, synthesis is the "ability to collect a disparate array of facts and connect them..." (Keene and Zimmerman 1997).

Mathematicians understand that a synthesis is the sum of information from new mathematical experiences and existing mathematical knowledge that leads to new ideas or understanding.

Students should understand that the process of synthesizing information requires a great deal of reflection on both old and new information, creativity and, quite often, sharing ideas with others. It is not a matter of simply consulting a textbook. Synthesis is the creative combining of information from various sources (Duffy 2003). By thinking and reflecting, blending ideas and testing the results, new and original ideas are generated.

Acquiring the ability to synthesize information is of tremendous value to the learner. As McGregor (2007) exhorts, "To be successful at any complex task requires the ability to synthesize." Explicitly teach this thinking strategy to prepare students for the future, wherever it may lead them.

Mathematicians know their knowledge of math continues to evolve as new information or ideas are encountered.

As students learn how to use synthesizing as a comprehension strategy, they begin to understand that synthesis may continue to evolve as they continue to explore and ponder. Not only may they find additional information or discover more relationships and patterns, but they may recall further existing knowledge that will modify their thinking.

Mathematicians can explain how using synthesis helps them better understand mathematics.

Students should be aware of how this strategy leads to better understanding of mathematics. They should be able to describe an example of synthesis leading to new understanding. The process of verbalizing their understanding helps students clarify their thinking about synthesis. Moreover, when they understand how and when to apply the strategy effectively, they are more likely to achieve the next step and actually apply it without prompting.

Teaching Students to Synthesize for Making Mathematical Meaning

Students may be capable of synthesizing when faced with familiar daily experiences, but struggle to apply the same strategy to mathematical understanding and problem solving. When they use it to understand real-life situations, it is done almost intuitively. They can seldom explain their thinking process as they generate new meaning in familiar contexts.

On the other hand, when they encounter new and unfamiliar information in what many students think of as a rigid discipline, they feel helpless and incapable of coming to grips with it. Help students first understand synthesis using concrete representations and then enable them to recognize how they use the process in everyday situations. This will lead students to employ this comprehension strategy in their mathematical explorations.

Modeling and Think-Alouds

It takes time to teach students to use and apply synthesis. Since it is a strategy that is critical for students to master if they are to become mathematical thinkers and develop deep conceptual understanding, use of the strategy must be explicitly taught. Because it is often difficult for students to grasp, teaching synthesis may require more modeling and think-alouds than any of the other strategies.

When teachers model synthesis in literacy lessons, they demonstrate how proficient readers pause every so often to think about what they are reading. As they pause, readers consider how each new piece of information enhances their understanding, allowing them to construct the meaning of the big ideas of the text. These big ideas are not the same as the main idea; instead, they are the overarching points of books, magazine articles, or arguments. As students learn to identify and converse with others about these big ideas, they build background knowledge that is valuable to understanding more challenging reading (Walmsley 2009).

In much the same way, students need to learn how to synthesize as they explore mathematics. They need to see how the many facets of mathematics with which they are working intermingle to form larger mathematical concepts—the big ideas. The more information students obtain from reflecting on their new experiences, the more their mathematical understanding expands.

In the following scenario, the teacher models the use of synthesis, and introduces a study of ratios. Basing the think-aloud on the reading of introductory materials about proportions, he demonstrates how by pausing and thinking, he understands their relationship to fractions.

> *As we begin exploring ratios today, I am going to model one of the comprehension strategies we are learning to use. I am going to use synthesis to give me a better understanding of ratios—going beyond the ideas in today's reading by reflecting*

and calling upon what I already know mathematically. Most of us have not yet learned about ratios, so it is very important that we build upon our prior knowledge. Stopping to think as I read helps me do that.

First, this lesson tells me that I will investigate two-color counters to show relationships between two quantities. So right away, I am trying to picture that in my mind. We have used these counters before to create representations of addition facts. I wonder if addition is related to ratios?

As I read on, I find out that ratios can be used to compare numbers in three ways depending on the situation. It shows a picture of two red counters and three yellow counters. In class, we have also used these counters to create models of fractional parts. Thinking about it that way, the two red counters are $\frac{2}{5}$ of the counters; the yellow counters are $\frac{3}{5}$ of the whole set. I wonder if ratios are related to fractions?

Now I'm looking at a table that shows that the red counters can be compared to all counters with a ratio of 2 to 5. That seems very much like thinking about fractional parts. Further in the chart, though, it says that you can compare all counters to the red counters for a ratio of 5 to 2. Let me think about how that compares to my understanding of fractions. Maybe if the two red counters were one set, each counter would be $\frac{1}{2}$ of the set. So, if I have five counters it represents $\frac{5}{2}$.

Next, the table says that ratios can be used to compare red counters to yellow counters with a ratio of 2 to 3. How in the world does that fit in with fractions? It might be like comparing $\frac{2}{5}$ to $\frac{3}{5}$. Or maybe it's like saying that if a whole set contains three counters like the yellow counters, the red set makes up $\frac{2}{3}$ of a set. Hmmm… I need to think about that some more.

After reading this lesson and looking at the illustrations and table, I think that there is a relationship between ratios and fractions. I need to find out more to better understand ratios.

To synthesize, I paused as I read to think about the new information in the reading and search my memory for things I already knew that might be related to the new ideas. Each time I read more, I learned a little more and reflected again. Although the reading didn't mention fractions, I was connecting ratios and fractions because of what I know about fractions. I need to explore ratios some more to get a better understanding. As I learn more, my synthesis will evolve and change.

Synthesizing is a valuable strategy to use when you are reading or working with new ideas in any subject area. Whenever you are reading or exploring new areas, be sure to pause and reflect frequently to expand your understanding. With this think-aloud, the teacher deliberately ended without a firm conclusion to the process of synthesis to demonstrate the ongoing, evolutionary nature of the strategy. Students need to see that the process continues, as does learning.

Most people give little thought to this process, so it is important to carefully plan lessons modeling the strategy. It is not always easy to break down the steps involved, but it is necessary for students to "see" how it is done.

Creating Concrete Experiences

Teaching students about this comprehension strategy can be difficult since it is so abstract. To infuse it with tangible meaning, introduce it using concrete objects.

Nesting Dolls

McGregor (2007) uses nesting dolls to launch her lessons on synthesis. Display each individual doll lined up in ascending order and begin the discussion by asking students how the nesting dolls could represent their thinking. Student responses typically suggest that their knowledge grows as they grow or that their thinking used to be one thing, but has changed over time. Students can be encouraged to share specific examples from their own experiences.

After students have been allowed to share their thinking, ask them to watch as the dolls are carefully put together, beginning with the smallest doll. Display the single doll and once again challenge students to compare this model to their thinking. With this concrete representation of synthesis, students begin to recognize that, like the doll, sometimes larger ideas or concepts are made up of many smaller ones that build up over time with new experiences.

Keep dolls on display throughout their study of synthesizing as a visual reference. This easily understood representation can be referred to whenever students need a reminder of what the strategy entails.

Baking a Cake

Harvey and Goudvis (2000) suggest baking a cake as a concrete example of synthesis. Students add each of the ingredients one by one and mix them. Help students realize that the separate ingredients that were added are now joined together to form the batter. The batter is poured into a pan and baked. When the warm cake emerges from the oven, encourage students to consider how the separate ingredients were mixed together to form a whole new food—just as when parts of stories all come together, they become the whole story.

To relate this experience to mathematics, make a similar analogy applicable to both understanding mathematical concepts and problems. As students explore mathematical ideas, and discover relationships and patterns, it is as if they are adding ingredients. Then, when they are able to make sense of the way these ideas are related to create a new understanding or revise their mathematical thinking, it is as if they can enjoy the finished cake.

These ideas can be used with students of any age. Whenever teachers are able to link a concept, especially an abstract concept, to a concrete item or experience, it becomes memorable and students are much more likely to retain it. Be resourceful in using other concrete objects as examples. Lego constructions, puzzles, peanut butter and jelly sandwiches, or, for the musically inclined, putting notes together to create a piece of music are all examples of joining parts together to construct a whole that is memorable for students.

Making Conjectures

Carpenter, Franke, and Levi begin their powerful book *Thinking Mathematically* (2003) with this statement:

> **"Learning mathematics involves learning ways of thinking. It involves learning powerful mathematical ideas rather than a collection of disconnected procedures for carrying out calculations. But it also entails learning how to generate those ideas, how to express them using words and symbols, and how to justify to oneself and to others that those ideas are true."**

Teachers are always searching for more effective methods of helping their students learn to think mathematically. Just how do students learn to generate those ideas? Generating those ideas requires that students focus on relationships and patterns they observe as they encounter mathematical ideas, and then apply what they already know to create new understandings. Basically, that is what young mathematicians do when they synthesize. As their syntheses continue to evolve, they examine their ideas in the light of new or newly recalled mathematical ideas and seek to justify to themselves that those ideas are true.

One of the most effective ways of promoting this kind of rigorous mathematical thinking is to provide opportunities for them to make conjectures—informed guesses and predictions based on observed patterns and relationships that appear to be true but that have not been tested. The NCTM (2000) Reasoning and Proof Standard states that all students should be able to "make and investigate mathematical conjectures." Furthermore, the Common Core State Standards (CCSS) for Mathematical Practice specify that students "make conjectures and build a logical progression of statements to explore the truth of their conjectures" (National Governors Association for Best Practices and Council of Chief State School Officers 2010).

While there is general agreement that making conjectures is an essential aspect of mathematics education, many teachers struggle with this idea. It may seem easier to explain mathematical concepts to students than to establish learning situations where students are expected to articulate and examine their mathematical thinking, and then make logical conjectures. In the long run, however, the mathematical thinking required to make conjectures, and the concepts students examine to make conjectures, lead them to deeper understandings about mathematics and enhances their ability to apply that knowledge to solve problems.

Students rarely make conjectures unless the process has been modeled and encouraged. Plan opportunities for students to explore examples of properties that lead them to create a conjecture. Provide students with a series of open number sentences and challenge them to determine if they are true or false (Carpenter, Franke, and Levi 2003). By recognizing patterns in these number sentences, students make conjectures about what might be true for any similar number sentence.

For example, to encourage students to develop a conjecture explaining the identity property of multiplication, ask students if the following number sentences are true or false:

$3{,}798 \times 1 = 3{,}779$

$23 \times 1 = 23$

$a \times 1 = 5$

$168 \times 0.1 = 168$

When students evaluate the validity of these following number sentences, a pattern should become clear and will allow them to make a conjecture about what happens when any number is multiplied by one. The student conjecture based on these true/false number sentences might include:

Whenever you multiply a number by one, the product equals the number you started with.

Students can explain why they believe this to be true and then test it to see if they can discover an exception. The conjecture may be posted in the classroom for revisiting and continued consideration.

- **Consider properties of number operations.**

These properties are critical ideas for both arithmetic and algebra. Because students create the conjectures about these properties, they are more likely to retain an understanding and be able to apply them appropriately. These properties include *identity*, *zero*, *inverse*, *commutative*, *associative*, and *distributive*.

- **Consider characteristics of special types of numbers.**

As students explore special kinds of numbers (e.g., odd/even, multiples of five, prime numbers, fractions, decimals, improper fractions), they can create conjectures about their characteristics. The more students explore these characteristics and state their observations verbally, the more likely these ideas are understood and internalized.

- **Consider procedural rules.**

Students may make conjectures about specific computational procedures. For example, they may state a rule for multiplying a decimal or for regrouping.

- **Make outcome predictions.**

Through conjecture, students predict the likely outcomes in mathematical situations. The category is one that must often be limited by certain conditions. Elementary students may conjecture that when numbers are added together, the sum is always greater than either number. Since the students are unfamiliar with negative numbers, explain that this conjecture is true for the numbers that they use for counting, but as they learn more about mathematics, they will find that there are other numbers for which this is not true.

Conjectures are an excellent example of synthesis at its best. Students consider their mathematics work combined with what they already know to understand more and take it a step further.

Math Stretches to Explore Synthesizing

The process of synthesis is quite complex and does not lend itself to Math Stretches as readily as some of the other comprehension strategies. Perhaps the most effective way to present a Math Stretch that addresses synthesis is to use a backward approach. Instead of asking students to create a synthesis, the synthesis or big mathematical idea is given. Students provide details that prove or disprove the given synthesis.

Support or Disprove This Conjecture Stretch

Post a chart titled "Support or Disprove This Conjecture." Students are directed to add a statement, numerical or verbal, that would support or disprove the given conjecture. They can add this directly to the chart or record it on a sticky note that they add to the chart. For example, the conjecture might be: *When you multiply two numbers, if you can change the order of the numbers you multiply, your product is the same.* When all students have responded, the class discusses the stretch in a Math Huddle. Use this Math Stretch a number of times, sometimes with conjectures that will prove to be true, but sometimes with conjectures that can be disproved. Student responses may include:

$5 \times 7 = 35$ and $7 \times 5 = 35$

$0 \times 1 = 0$ and $1 \times 0 = 1$

$567 \times 10 = 5,670$ and $10 \times 567 = 5,670$

As students respond to this stretch, some may multiply the first number sentence, but since they understand this property of multiplication, they simply use the same product in the second number sentence. Other students who have not completely grasped the concept will multiply both number sentences. In the light of trying to verify the conjecture, that is probably the more reasonable choice. The Math Huddle provides an excellent opportunity to explore these ideas.

In the Context of Problem Solving

Problem solving is one of the most effective ways to teach students mathematical concepts. Contrary to the traditional approach to teaching mathematics in the United States where a concept is taught by the teacher and then students attempt to apply it in a problem-solving scenario, the more effective instructional approach is to teach the concept through problem solving.

This approach is addressed in the NCTM Problem-Solving Standards (2000), which state that students should be capable of "building mathematical knowledge through problem solving." Students are given the responsibility of learning from their experiences. Similarly, the CCSS for Mathematical Practice (NGABP and CCSSO 2010) specify that when problem-solving, students "make conjectures about the form and meaning of the solution.... They consider analogous problems, and try special cases and simpler forms of the original problem in order to gain insight into its solution." Students must draw upon their background knowledge, and through the process of mathematizing as they interact with the problem, develop new mathematical understandings. In other words, students are expected to use the comprehension strategy of synthesis as they make sense of the problem. Well-conceived problems give students the opportunity to solidify their understanding and to extend what they know (NCTM 2000).

Hiebert et al. (1997) emphasize the importance of providing students the chance to learn from their attempts to solve problems. "We believe that if we want students to understand mathematics, it is more helpful to think of understanding as something that results from solving problems, rather than something we can teach them directly."

Approaches to problem solving change considerably when teachers think of understanding as an outcome of problem solving rather than something that is taught directly. Instead of an assessment tool, measuring students' ability to apply previously taught math concepts, the focus shifts and teachers consider what mathematical relationships students will take with them from the problem-solving experience. The teacher becomes a facilitator, responsible for guiding students' mathematical journeys and for establishing a classroom environment conducive to *mathematizing*, one in which students are honored as thinkers and mathematics is a living discipline.

Choose problems from which students can learn. This is an extremely important task. Frequently, word problems are little more than glorified number sentences, giving students scant opportunities to extend their mathematical understanding. Problems should be open, with a diverse set of possible solutions, and allow students to identify relationships, discover patterns, and make conjectures. Problems should be interesting enough that students pose additional questions—what ifs.

Encourage students to share problem-solving strategies to extend their understanding further and have it evolve during classroom discussions.

Using Children's Literature

Many students are accustomed to synthesizing during reading, so using children's literature is a fitting method to teach this strategy for mathematical comprehension. Through stories, students experience mathematics in "real" situations. The mathematical circumstances usually unfold bit by bit, encouraging pauses and reflection.

In choosing texts to connect with mathematics, look for more than just an entertaining story or a high-interest nonfiction text—although any text used for mathematics should certainly have those characteristics. Consider the following questions (O'Connell 2007):

- **Is the book or article of an appropriate reading/listening level for students?**

Determine whether the text will be read aloud to students, read independently by students, or both. If using a hard-copy of the book, select a big book with large text and pictures. If using an interactive whiteboard, consider ebooks that can be easily viewed by students. With read-alouds, the use of a slightly higher reading and listening level allows scaffolding. Unfamiliar vocabulary is clarified, and pausing throughout the story lets students review what has occurred.

- **Does the math fit with the lesson?**

Some texts have obvious mathematical connections. Be resourceful to find mathematical connections in texts that are not directly math-related. Although these are sometimes discovered spontaneously when reading aloud (and should certainly be discussed, if appropriate), review the texts and identify mathematical teaching points prior to using them with students in an instructional situation.

- **Is the text engaging?**

Student engagement is one of the major advantages to using literature to teach mathematics. Any fiction or nonfiction text should capture students' interests enough to encourage mathematical thinking. Be aware of student interests and choose texts that align with those interests.

- **Do you enjoy the book?**

A teacher's enjoyment of a story is obvious as he or she reads it aloud, and students pick up on it. The more engaged the teacher, the more engaged the students, and the more likely they are to become engaged in the lesson. If there are times when student book choices and your interests are not aligned, consider reading them anyway and graciously hide your lack of interest.

When using children's literature to teach students about synthesizing, most of the instruction occurs during and after the reading. Throughout the read-aloud, pause to ask probing questions that help students identify the mathematical relationships in the text and make connections to their own experiences and mathematical knowledge. Students can be encouraged to identify the overall mathematical ideas related to the text and how they are connected. Include "What if...?" questions to extend student thinking. The strategy that is taught and implemented during the read-aloud should be discussed explicitly. How is it applied? In what ways is the use of synthesis creating greater understanding?

In the following example, synthesis is taught through the book *365 Penguins* by Fromental and Jolivet (2006). On New Year's Day, penguins begin to be mysteriously delivered to a family—one each day. The family has no idea where they are coming from, but the number of penguins quickly becomes overwhelming. The family devises numerous ways to cope with the burgeoning number of penguins who now live with them.

Throughout the text, various sets are explored. The family had received seven penguins after a week, and 31 at the end of the month. In an attempt to organize them, they create sets of 15, which works until another penguin shows up. At one point, they store a dozen in each drawer. The family computes the cost of feeding the penguins using multiplication. The mathematical references continue as this humorous story progresses.

In this discussion, the teacher wants the students to reflect on how the mathematical references in the text relate and to generate a synthesis.

Teacher: *Did you enjoy this book as much as I did?*

Stan: *There were too many penguins. I can't imagine that. My house is much too small to hold all those penguins.*

Teacher: *Can we think about this story for a few minutes? We have been learning how to use synthesis to help us understand mathematical relationships. During the story, we stopped to reflect on the relationships. You had great observations. Let's add these to our chart.*

Rayshun: *They got one penguin every day—that's 365 penguins in a year. We would know that even if they didn't tell us because we know there are 365 days in a year.*

Mandy: *And, they got seven penguins after a week. One week has seven days.*

Teacher: *Stop a minute and reflect. What kinds of relationships are those? Do you see any patterns or connections?*

Stan: *They are all about time periods—days, weeks, years. Oh—and months are on our chart, too. So I see a pattern there. They are all chunks of time.*

Teacher: *Those are great observations. We are synthesizing the information. What else do we see on our chart that we observed as we read?*

Mandy: *They put a dozen penguins in each drawer.*

Rayshun: *The dad put them in groups of 15 when they had 60 penguins.*

Geoff: *Penguins eat 2.5 pounds of fish every day!*

Teacher: *Let's stop again and think. A few minutes ago, we noticed that many of the mathematical relationships in the book had to do with time periods. We've discussed this further; do you think that applies to the mathematical references you just named?*

Stan: *No, they don't have anything to do with time.*

Teacher: *Do you notice anything that they all have in common?*

Geoff: *They all have to do with groups, don't they? Not necessarily time, but groups of things.*

Mandy: *Right—a group of days, a group of fish—well, pounds anyway.*

Stan: *And, a dozen is a group. Just like the groups of 15.*

Teacher: *So, you think that maybe the overall mathematical idea of this book is examining groups or sets of things?*

Rayshun: *Maybe we should look at the rest of the things on the chart to see if it works for all of them.*

Teacher: *You are using the information from the book with what you know mathematically to create a synthesis—just as mathematicians do. Our synthesis evolved and changed as we considered additional information. And, Rayshun, what you just said makes so much sense! Whenever we create a synthesis, we need to continue trying to check to see if it is true or whether it will evolve even further. I am so impressed with your mathematical thinking today!*

During this read-aloud discussion, the questions led students to reflect and focus on the mathematical ideas they noticed in the story. Beyond simply reviewing those ideas, students were challenged to synthesize the information by looking for relationships and patterns to see commonalities—to find the big mathematical idea of the story.

Chapter Snapshot

Because of its complexity, synthesis is often difficult to teach and requires students to be familiar with the comprehension strategies addressed in earlier chapters. Ellin Keene (Keene and Zimmermann 1997) made it clear that to her, synthesis is of the utmost importance to learning as she wrote:

"I realize now that synthesis is absolutely basic—in the air and water category—if we are talking about essentials for learning: literacy learning, life learning. The magnitude and complexity of the information we and the children with whom we work must manage is staggering....In order to construct any kind of meaning in our literacy learning and life learning, we must find ways to cull and prune the details with which we are bombarded. We must reorganize and create our own definitions of what we our learning, our own definitions of our lives at any particular juncture."

Although her focus was clearly on literacy learning, this is also true for mathematical learning. Students may be "taught" the mathematics curriculum, but unless they are able to recognize the big mathematical ideas, see how the details relate to the big ideas, and apply these to real-life situations, they are not mathematically literate.

Students deserve the opportunity to delve more deeply into the discipline of mathematics, to become more than procedurally proficient. Learning how to apply the strategy of synthesis to their study of mathematics, prepares students to assume responsibility for their own learning. They become aware that understanding mathematics is more than just knowing facts and procedures. They discover that "Mathematics is a science of concepts and processes that have a pattern of regularity and logical order. Finding and exploring this regularity of order, and then making sense of it, is what mathematics is all about" (Van de Walle, Karp, and Bay-Williams 2010).

Review and Reflect

1. Think about the process of synthesis. In your own words, how do you define it?

2. Reflect on a time in your life, either academic or personal, when you have used the strategy of synthesis to gain a better understanding of something. How did you apply the process? In what ways did it increase your understanding? What can you take from your reflections to improve the way you teach your students to synthesize?

3. Choose a piece of math-related children's literature. Plan a lesson on synthesis based on the read-aloud of this text. What synthesis questions can you use to help students identify the big idea?

Chapter 9

Monitoring Mathematical Comprehension

A hallmark of expert readers is the ability to actively and continuously make meaning as they read. If meaning begins to break down, they are able to quickly recognize it and apply strategies to repair their wavering comprehension (Wilhelm 2001). In like fashion, monitoring for meaning occurs naturally for proficient mathematicians. Similar to the way Keene and Zimmerman (2007) describe proficient readers, these mathematicians "listen to inner voices, make ongoing corrections and adjustments, and are aware of how meaning evolves." The process is often subconscious and seamless.

Unfortunately, this is not the case for many students. Some students are simply unaware of whether or not they understand the mathematics with which they are working, and, moreover, they do not expect to understand it. Others may recognize their confusion, but lack the fix-up strategies they need to remedy it.

Monitoring and repairing comprehension requires an amalgamation of the comprehension strategies described in this book. It is an umbrella term under which the others fall (Keene and Zimmerman 2007). Each of the strategies is, in fact, an element of the monitoring process. Interlaced, they provide a platform for understanding and interpreting new ideas. This strategy might well be the first or last of the strategies to be taught.

Keene and Zimmerman (2007) suggest that teachers kick off the school year with a short unit on monitoring comprehension that emphasizes "the importance of revising our thinking as we read, being metacognitive, and paying attention so we know when we're understanding and when we're not, and can do something about it." The obvious disadvantage to using this unit in the beginning of the year is the lack of strategies students can draw upon to help them monitor and repair understanding. When it is the last of the strategies to be taught, students already have a toolbox of additional comprehension strategies to use as they monitor their understanding and repair meaning when needed.

Regardless of when teachers choose to introduce and teach this strategy, each of the comprehension strategies provides students with unique, yet overlapping ways of monitoring and repairing comprehension. Students, as they apply these strategies, learn to automatically monitor and revise their thinking as they read or work with mathematical ideas. Thus, even if monitoring meaning as a strategy is not taught until after the other strategies have been introduced, students are still engaged in monitoring and repairing comprehension throughout the school year.

Metacognition

According to Van de Walle, Karp, and Bay-Williams (2010), metacognition "refers to conscious monitoring (an awareness of how and why you are doing something) and regulation (choosing to do something or deciding to make changes) of your own thought processes." In other words, we monitor our own thinking. To do so requires us to regularly think about our thinking.

Literacy research shows that effective readers are metacognitively active as they read. The ability to monitor one's comprehension is what distinguishes good readers from poor readers. Proficient readers are able to self-correct and repair comprehension problems as they read. Their goal is to understanding the big ideas of a text. "By reading and then accepting, adapting, or rejecting what they have learned, they have entered into the grand social conversation that is reading, not only the reading of texts, but of using texts to 'read' the world" (Wilhelm 2001).

But many low-achieving readers lack metacognitive awareness. They are unaware that they should monitor their own understanding and be in control of their own reading comprehension. These students fail to assess their comprehension as they read and have inadequate strategies to fix or repair their comprehension (Taylor et al. 1994).

More metacognitively sophisticated readers, however, know how to extract meaning from print. They are aware of their thinking processes in the moment and over the long term. In the moment, they focus on whether the text itself is understood; for the long term, they know what strategies to draw upon to enhance comprehension and are instinctively aware of when those strategies should be applied. They react to confusion by employing a wealth of fix-up strategies, including, but not limited to, asking questions, constructing images, and summarizing (Pressley 2002).

Proficient mathematicians employ the same strategies as they explore new mathematical ideas. The NCTM (2000) standard for problem solving states that students should be able to "monitor and reflect on the process of mathematics problem solving." As part of the process of problem solving, students should constantly monitor and adjust their mathematical thinking and processes. The CCSS (2010) Standards for Mathematical Practice also emphasize the importance of monitoring and evaluating progress and changing course if or when necessary. Students should recognize the importance of monitoring the reasonableness of their mathematical work by asking, "Does this make sense?" Clearly, to be considered proficient in mathematics, as in reading, students need to be able to monitor their understanding and have fix-up strategies that allow them to successfully self-correct when necessary.

Monitoring Understanding for Mathematics Learners

During their school years, students are expected to develop a deep conceptual understanding of mathematics and with it the ability to effectively and efficiently apply those concepts to problem solving. To be successful at either of these endeavors, students must learn how to reflectively and critically examine their own thinking to ensure that they understand major mathematical concepts and, when engaged in problem solving, thoroughly understand the problems to be solved. Thus, monitoring for meaning in mathematics has a dual focus.

Conceptual Understanding

The first step of monitoring for meaning in mathematics is monitoring conceptual understanding. Unfortunately, with traditional mathematics instruction, little worth was given to the conceptual understanding of students. Fosnot and Dolk (2001) describe what they call "school mathematics," which is very different from the work of mathematicians in the real world. In the isolated and limited world of "school mathematics," the teacher plays the role of "the fountain of wisdom who understood that mathematics was a discipline thought to comprise facts, skills, concepts, formulas, and algorithms, and this discipline could be transmitted, explained, practiced, and learned if teachers were well versed in it and learners were diligent."

Students saw mathematics as something to be explained by the teacher, practiced with guidance, and then applied to problems with familiar and predictable formats. Most often, especially in elementary school, students were expected to learn the procedures needed to carry out computations, but were rarely expected to understand the mathematical concepts behind the procedures. Much like the way struggling readers tend to focus on decoding words and lose track of meaning, too many mathematics students focused on procedures rather than on mathematical meaning.

Consequently, students believed that they were not responsible for mathematical understanding, only for their ability to plug in numbers to the correct algorithms and calculate the answers with accuracy. If they were able to do this, by their way of thinking, they were mathematically proficient. This view resulted in large numbers of students who failed to retain the knowledge of mathematics that they had "learned" and who were also unable to apply what they did know to solving problems in unfamiliar contexts.

The first step in helping students learn how to monitor their mathematical understanding is leading them to see that learning mathematics requires them to take responsibility for their own understanding. Tovani (2000) describes her initial shock when one of her middle school students blurted out that he was "sick and tired of you telling the class that it's our job to know when we don't know. You're the teacher. Aren't you the one who is supposed to know when we understand something and when we don't?" He went on to add, "How am I supposed to know when I don't know something? I'm just a kid."

Many students share that attitude about the role of teachers—not only regarding reading comprehension, but mathematics comprehension as well. Students only too gladly relinquish that responsibility to their teachers—although reading the minds of their students to know whether or not they understand is clearly an impossible task.

Demonstrate respect for students by asking them to shoulder the responsibility for monitoring their understanding and to take appropriate steps to repair comprehension when necessary. They should know and apply fix-up strategies when meaning breaks down. Pose explicit questions such as: *How do you know whether or not you understand? What do you do if you are confused?*

In some respects, teaching students how to monitor their mathematical understanding may be a more challenging task than it is with reading comprehension. Although poor readers may not expect to understand what they are reading, there is still a general consensus that reading entails more than just word calling. Students, for the most part, realize that they are expected to understand what they read, even if they lack confidence in the ability to do it.

With mathematics, however, there is a prevailing attitude among students, and sometimes parents, that procedural knowledge and fact fluency are evidence of mathematical proficiency. Teachers have to educate students and parents on how imperative it is that students also achieve conceptual understanding and the ability to monitor that understanding.

Problem Solving

The second part of the dual focus of monitoring mathematical comprehension relates to problem solving. Conceptual understanding forms the underpinning of problem-solving competence. The comprehension necessary for successful problem solving, however, goes beyond the comprehension of the mathematical concepts. Too often, students plunge into problem solving without understanding the meaning of the problems. Without this understanding, problem-solving attempts by students are little more than guessing games.

Prior to even considering the mathematical knowledge necessary to solve the problem, students must be able to read and interpret the problem. To do this, they should be able to visualize the scenario, identify the facts and details of the problem, and discern exactly what it is they are asked to find. It is no wonder that Pólya (1957) considered understanding the problem to be the first phase in problem solving.

Many times, mathematics teachers must assume the role of a reading teacher to help their students strategically approach the task of reading problems for understanding. Struggling students tend to focus on decoding words in the problems, rather than on establishing the overall meaning of the problem. They may randomly choose one or two words on which to base their problem-solving approach without ever having a clear understanding of the meaning of the problem. Instructional time is well-spent on helping these students decipher problems as well as teaching problem-solving strategies.

Once students grasp the contexts of the problems they are to solve, they can progress to the second of Pólya's (1957) problem-solving steps—making a plan. For this step, they must "see how the various items are connected, how the unknown is linked to the data, in order to obtain the idea of the solution." Integral to this plan is an understanding of the problem and the mathematical concepts required to solve it.

Pólya goes on to warn that "the worst may happen if the student embarks upon computations or constructions without having *understood* the problem. It is generally useless to carry out details without having seen the main connections, or having made a sort of plan." Thus, to solve problems successfully, having a clear understanding of both the problem and the related mathematical concepts is crucial. Students need to consciously monitor their comprehension of both and work to repair that understanding whenever necessary.

What Students Need to Know about Monitoring and Repairing Mathematical Comprehension

Experienced mathematicians constantly monitor their mathematical understanding, just as proficient readers reflect and monitor their reading comprehension (Tovani 2000). Student need to know that:

1. Mathematicians know it is their job to monitor comprehension as they explore mathematical ideas and solve problems. As they work, they reflect on their mathematical thinking. They know when it makes sense.

2. Mathematicians know when they do not understand and take steps to repair their comprehension. They do not disguise or ignore their confusion.

3. Mathematicians know how to identify their confusion so they can fix up their understanding.

4. Mathematicians call upon fix-up strategies to help them understand the mathematics when their comprehension breaks down.

5. Mathematicians use fix-up strategies flexibly. When one does not work, they try another.

Mathematicians know it is their job to monitor comprehension as they explore mathematical ideas and solve problems. As they work, they reflect on their mathematical thinking. They know when it makes sense.

Students should assume responsibility for monitoring their understanding of both the mathematical concepts and the problem-solving contexts with which they are working. With targeted instruction, their effectiveness at monitoring their comprehension increases, and as a result they show improvement in problem solving (Van de Walle, Karp, and Bay-Williams 2010). Students should be metacognitively active whenever they are engaged in mathematical work—continuously reviewing their experiences and "identifying points of confusion, the level of certainty they have about content preconceptions that were accurate and preconceptions that were inaccurate" (Marzano 2007). Students should understand that in order to maximize their mathematical success, they must recognize when mathematical meaning eludes them.

Mathematicians know when they do not understand and take steps to repair their comprehension. They do not disguise or ignore their confusion.

When cognitive breakdowns occur, students should know to apply fix-up strategies to help them repair and construct meaning. In mathematics, as in reading, low-achieving students often continue with their mathematical work even when they have no understanding of its meaning. When this occurs, they may be successful at computations and less rigorous mathematical tasks, but these students fail to develop the deep conceptual foundation that is essential for future mathematical success.

Mathematicians know how to identify their confusion so they can fix up their understanding.

Once they realize that their understanding has broken down, students need to know how to pinpoint exactly when and where it happened. Students should know that the study of mathematics requires reflection—especially when they realize that they are not sure if they understand the concepts or problems. They must be able to analyze the cause of their confusion. When they identify the breakdown in understanding, they can effectively address it by employing appropriate fix-up strategies to repair comprehension.

Mathematicians call upon fix-up strategies to help them understand the mathematics when their comprehension breaks down.

Students should have a repertoire of strategies at hand that they can apply to restore comprehension. Help students develop a variety of methods to address the different kinds of problems they may encounter as they learn mathematics and solve problems. These strategies should be explicitly taught and then practiced by students.

Mathematicians use fix-up strategies flexibly. When one does not work, they try another.

Help students learn to consciously select the best strategies to clarify the mathematical ideas that they are having trouble understanding. According to Keene and Zimmerman (2007), using fix-up strategies requires that students be flexible, adaptive, and independent. They are flexible in that they have an array of possible strategies from which to choose. Their adaptability allows them to focus on the tool or strategy that is most likely to be effective in any specific situation. And, finally, they learn to independently solve comprehension problems. As evidence of their flexibility, adaptability, and independence, they are able to try a strategy, assess its effectiveness, and then try another strategy if needed.

Repairing Comprehension

Tovani (2000) compares monitoring understanding and using fix-up strategies to driving a car. When driving, we have a destination in mind and are always conscious of what is going on in and around the car. We monitor the car's speed, its fuel level, and surrounding traffic. If a problem occurs, we stop to resolve it. If a tire goes flat, we decide on the best way to deal with it—changing the tire or calling for assistance. Either way, the tire must be fixed before driving on.

Just as drivers have a destination, mathematicians expect to understand the math they are learning. The purpose is to make mathematical meaning; if meaning breaks down, it must be repaired before moving on. Students should view comprehension breakdowns as part of the learning process, not as failure. When they recognize that mathematicians are constantly making meaning as they grapple with new ideas, students are more willing to admit when they are confused and to apply fix-up strategies.

It often helps students to have a comprehension checklist (figure 9.1 below and Appendix F) to guide them as they reflect on their own learning. This checklist provides a clear structure for remembering the importance of monitoring their comprehension.

Fig. 9.1. Comprehension Checklist

---

1. Get ready to think mathematically
- ❑ scan texts for illustrations, diagrams, and text features
- ❑ consider your purpose for the mathematical work
- ❑ reflect on what you already know about the concept or problem

2. Monitor your comprehension as you work
- ❑ notice what you do not understand
- ❑ apply fix-up strategies

3. Improve your comprehension as you work
- ❑ make connections
- ❑ ask questions
- ❑ visualize
- ❑ make inferences or predictions
- ❑ determine what is important
- ❑ synthesize

4. Check your comprehension again as you complete your work
- ❑ explain your understanding in your own words
- ❑ check that your solution makes sense

(Adapted from Taylor et al. 1994)

Students need specific instruction to recognize when they are confused.

Give them a set of clues that can alert them when their comprehension is wavering. These are some signs that students should heed (adapted from Tovani 2000):

- **Your internal voice is not interacting mathematically with the concept or problem.**

  When a student focuses on what is given and has no inner voice making connections, asking questions, or making inferences, he or she is failing to make meaning.

- **You are unable to visualize the mathematical concept or problem.**

  This is an indication that the student should reflect and engage in fix-up work.

- **Your mind wanders away from the mathematical work at hand.**

  It is time to pause and refocus.

- **You are unable to recall the details of a math idea or problem.**

  Go back to rethink the mathematical task.

- **You cannot find answers to the questions asked to clarify meaning.**

  Comprehension has broken down and needs to be repaired.

When students recognize that they do not understand, they need to have reliable strategies they can apply to repair their understanding.

Share some of your own comprehension problems and how you address them. Encourage them to share when they were confused about math and what they did to overcome their confusion. Since monitoring and repairing comprehension are literacy strategies, students may make comparisons to literacy fix-up strategies. As students brainstorm fix-up strategies, record their ideas on chart paper and display for future reference. See figure 9.2 for a list of possible fix-up strategies.

Fig. 9.2. Mathematical Fix-Up Strategies

When I get confused, I can...
- think about my mathematical purpose
- identify any unfamiliar vocabulary
- reread the mathematical text or problems
- look for text features or text structure to give me any clues
- ask myself questions
- connect to other mathematical concepts I know
- relate personal experiences I have had
- visualize the problem
- draw a diagram to represent the problem
- use manipulatives
- try to restate it in my own words
- think of a similar problem
- try a different problem-solving approach
- talk with another student
- ask someone for help

(Adapted from Owocki 2003 and O'Connell 2007)

A repertoire of fix-up strategies gives students the confidence to tackle challenging academic endeavors. They learn that a breakdown in understanding is not unusual, and they are prepared to deal with it.

Teaching Students to Monitor Mathematical Understanding

Math teachers notice struggling students (adapted from Wilhelm 2001):

- plow right through their work with little, if any, conceptual understanding

- do not recognize meaningful mathematical connections and relationships

- give up easily

Teaching these students how to examine their levels of understanding and how to strengthen that understanding when it wanes eliminates the helpless feeling many of them face. In addition to providing scaffolding to the struggling learner, these skills benefit all learners, making them more reflective and resourceful—and, as a result, they become bolder, less passive students.

Modeling and Think-Alouds

Teacher modeling of monitoring understanding and the use of fix-up strategies is particularly important. Students are predisposed to equate lack of understanding with being "dumb" and with failure. When they are confused, some continue as if mathematical understanding were not essential; others just give up. It is essential for them to realize that mathematicians view confusion or a breakdown in comprehension as a challenge. They dig deeper to find a way to make sense of the mathematics that is confusing to them. Use modeling and think-alouds to convey that important message to students.

In the following vignette, the teacher is sharing his experience when he first began multiplying whole numbers by fractions. The products he generated did not make sense to him.

Today, we are learning how important it is to reflect on our understanding of the math we are studying. Let me share something that happened to me when I was in school. We had studied multiplication of whole numbers. I thought I was pretty smart! I just knew that whenever you multiplied two numbers, the product would be greater than either of the numbers.

Well, the class was just beginning to learn about multiplying a whole number by a fraction. At first, I listened well to the teacher's directions. I was sure I knew what I was doing, so I just sort of tuned out while she finished explaining the process. She assigned us a set of problems to complete that she wrote on the board.

I wrote them down and began work. The first one was:

$$\tfrac{1}{2} \times 2 = ?$$

I followed the procedures she had explained to us. My answer was 1. Wait a minute! I was totally confused. Had I worked the problem incorrectly? I was sure the product had to be more than 2.

At first, I thought I would just go on and act as if I understood it. But, the more I thought about it, I knew that either I had worked the problem incorrectly or else what I thought I understood about multiplication was not true all the time. In other words, I was monitoring my understanding—and I discovered that I was confused.

Unfortunately, when I was in school, we never talked about what to do if you get confused. I was scared to let my teacher know that I was confused. I didn't know that it is good to think about what you do and don't understand—that it helps you learn when you figure out something. I wish I had had this chart of fix-up strategies to try.

Finally, I decided to draw an array to see what was going on. How was I going to draw half a row? I thought about it and then drew half circles to represent half a row. Since there were two columns, I drew two half circles. That was $\frac{1}{2} \times 2$. When I looked at it, I realized I had been mistaken in thinking that a product was always going to be greater than either of the factors. I could see the product really was two halves or 1. I still wasn't sure why, but I decided it must be correct. I used the fix-up strategy of drawing a diagram. Even then, I still didn't want to let my teacher know I was a little confused.

If I had just gone ahead and not thought about it, I would not have understood multiplication by fractions as quickly. After that, I listened carefully so I could figure this out.

When you are working with mathematical ideas or with problem solving, really think about how well you understand what you are doing. If you find you are confused, try some of the fix-up strategies to see if everything makes sense. That's a great process to go through. It makes you true mathematicians.

If you are still confused, let me know, and we can work on it together. There are probably other students in the class who are also confused.

The teacher think-aloud in this vignette was not a conventional think-aloud. Rather than describing thinking going on in the present, the teacher shares the thinking involved in a past learning experience. Since the experience was that of a student, the class readily identified with it.

Huh?

Harvey and Goudvis (2007) stress "how important it is for teachers to realize when kids are confused and to help them do something about it." This idea is an adaptation of one of their instructional ideas, "Knowing When You Know and Knowing When You Don't Know." They noticed when students did not understand something they were reading, they would wrinkle their noses and say, "Huh?" Accordingly, they suggest that students who are confused place a sticky note labeled "Huh?" at the confusing section of the text. Later if the confusion is clarified, students add a light bulb to the note. When teachers circulate around the room and confer with their students, they know the parts of the text they should discuss.

This adaptation of that instructional strategy also encourages students to monitor their understanding. Students create tri-fold displays from tag board. They label one side "Huh?" and, on the other side, draw a picture of a light bulb. Working individually or in groups, students are reminded that they are responsible for monitoring their understanding. If comprehension is fine, they display the light bulb. When comprehension breaks down, they display "Huh?"

Scan the room to assess the level of understanding. If large numbers of students are displaying "Huh?" it may be time to ask students to pause in their work and meet together to clarify meaning. Otherwise, confer with those students who indicate a breakdown in understanding, while the others continue to work uninterrupted. This approach to monitoring comprehension prompts students to do regular comprehension checks, lets students know that it is okay to be confused, and provides teachers with an informal visual assessment of student understanding.

Ticket Out the Door Comprehension Check

It is not unusual for teachers to use Tickets Out the Door for the purpose of formative assessment. At the end of a class, ask students to explain their understanding of a concept, answer a question, complete a calculation, or solve a problem and hand the work in as a "ticket out the door." Then, use this work to assess student understanding of the day's lesson and to inform instruction for the following day.

Take the Ticket Out the Door a step further by asking students to rate their level of understanding. Categories might include: "I'm crystal clear," "It's a bit hazy," and "I'm in a fog!" (McGregor 2007). This self-assessment by students serves two purposes. First, students are reminded of the importance of monitoring their understanding and are even required to do so. Second, some students who have responded to the "ticket out the door" question correctly may still feel confused about the math content. Using the Ticket Out the Door, they are able to share their confusion with the teacher. Conference with those students to identify the source of confusion. In addition, some students may have responded with an incorrect answer, but indicate that they have a clear understanding. Meet with those students to discover the reason for the discrepancy.

Comprehension Constructor

After students know how to assess their own understanding, can recognize areas of confusion, and utilize a variety of fix-up strategies, they can try a Comprehension Constructor (figure 9.3 and Appendix G) to structure their independent thinking. Adapted from Tovani's (2000) Comprehension Constructor for reading comprehension, this organizer provides scaffolding for students' initial attempts at building meaning through the use of fix-up strategies by helping them focus on the source of their confusion and creating a plan to construct meaning.

Fig. 9.3. Comprehension Constructor

I am confused by:
_____
This is what I am thinking:
_____
I will try this fix-up strategy:
_____
Now I understand:
_____
I am still confused and need some help to understand:
_____

(Adapted from Tovani 2000)

Before students are expected to complete this form on their own, it should be introduced during whole-class or small-group instruction. Clearly explain the expectations for each line and provide several completed forms as exemplars. Students will need help in learning to describe their confusion in specific, rather than general, terms. Monitor the forms on a regular basis. If students indicate that they are still confused, more instruction may be needed to clarify the mathematical ideas or problems or to help the students identify more strategies for repairing meaning.

Once students begin using these forms to assist in creating meaning, encourage them to share and compare them with others in the class. The discussion generated may highlight other appropriate fix-up strategies.

Using Math Stretches for Monitoring Comprehension

Many of the Math Stretches described in this book and the Math Stretch series indirectly encourage students to examine their understanding of various mathematical concepts and problems. During the Math Huddles, encourage students to share any breakdown in understanding that they discover when responding to the stretch or during the ensuing discourse. As a natural follow-up, discuss the fix-up strategies that might be applied to clarify and increase understanding.

Color-Code Metacognition Math Stretch

When students are familiar with this comprehension strategy, they can be expected to demonstrate their ability to reflect and assess their own learning. At this time, assign the Color-Code Metacognition Math Stretch. It may be used to address comprehension of either mathematical concepts or of word problems.

The stretch challenges students to reflect on a math concept or a word problem and rate their understanding of it using colored sticky notes. If students feel as if they have a good understanding, they choose a green sticky note, write a statement about the concept or problem that shows understanding, initial it, and add it to the chart. If they somewhat understand it, they choose a yellow sticky note, write a statement about possible confusion, initial it, and add it to the chart. Students who feel they are very confused about the topic or problem choose an orange sticky note, write a specific statement about their confusion, initial it, and add it to the chart.

With traditional mathematics instruction, students may have been reluctant to admit a lack of understanding. To encourage students to accurately self-assess their understanding, students are praised as they freely share their reflections and suggestions for fix-up strategies.

One glance at the chart gives a graphic picture of the overall understanding of the class. A sea of green indicates that only a few individuals or one small group are confused. On the other hand, a sea of orange sticky notes indicates that the whole class may need more learning opportunities.

In the Context of Problem Solving

According to Van de Walle, Karp, and Bay-Williams (2010), "the key to success is being intentional and consciously developing the metacognitive skills to monitor and reflect on the problems being solved." Students must understand the problems, as well as the strategies and the mathematical concepts needed to solve them. They should be taught that monitoring understanding when solving problems includes examining their knowledge in each of those areas.

Metacognitive reflection is valuable in all phases of problem solving: before, during, and after.

- **Before Phase:** As they consider a problem, students must understand both the context of the problem and what it is they are being asked to find. They must read slowly and delve into meaning, chunk by chunk—reading a little, thinking a little (Murphy 2010), and rereading to clarify meaning.

  When they are confident that they understand the problem scenario and question, they must decide which are the important facts to help solve it. Then they must consider the appropriate strategies to use and plan how to arrive at a solution. Pólya's (1957) problem-solving framework shows that students complete two steps: they understand the problem and plan how to solve it. If understanding breaks down during this phase, they should use a fix-up strategy.

- **During Phase:** Students continue to use various comprehension strategies to monitor understanding and revise when needed. They consider the plan they have made as they implement it, questioning what they are doing, why they are doing it, and how it is helping them.

  In the During Phase, students complete the third step of Pólya's framework, carrying out the plan. Here, Pólya warns that "teachers must insist that the student should *check each step*." Students need to be convinced of the correctness of each problem-solving step.

  In some situations, students lose their conviction that their plan is working. It is important that students recognize the flexibility that is required when solving challenging problems. Emphasize that flexibility leads to more productive problem solving. Students should not feel constrained by the first problem-solving plan they try. If those strategies prove to be ineffective, students should know to revisit their plan and try another tactic. Too often, students decide on a problem-solving strategy, and then rigidly stick with it whether or not it is successful.

- **After Phase:** If they feel finished because they have found the answer, students may be tempted to skip this phase. But students should consider whether their solutions make sense. This step is too frequently overlooked. Encourage students to convince peers of the reasonableness of their answers. Demonstrate the value of continued self-monitoring by having students justify their answers and discuss how they arrived at their answers in whole-class or small-group settings.

It is in the After Phase that the fourth step of Pólya's problem-solving framework is carried out—looking back at the completed solution with review and discussion. Pólya states, "By looking back at the completed solution, by reconsidering and reexamining the result and the path that led to it, they [students] could consolidate their knowledge and develop their ability to solve problems." He urged teachers to impress on students that no problem is ever completely exhausted. With sufficient thought, any solution can be improved, as can student understanding of the solution.

Using Children's Literature

Because of the close relationship between comprehension instruction in literacy and in mathematics, using children's literature to teach the importance of monitoring mathematical comprehension is ideal. Read-alouds offer teachers opportunities to model and think aloud as they monitor student understanding when reading mathematical texts and when solving problems. Moreover, the appeal of children's literature is universal. Mathematical ideas presented in literary form inspire student thinking.

Using Tang's book, *The Grapes of Math: Mind-Stretching Math Riddles* (2001), this teacher models how to monitor understanding while reading a math-related text.

> *How many of you enjoy trying to figure out the answers to riddles? I love it! Today, we are reading a book by Greg Tang about "mind-stretching math riddles." It sounds like it will be a challenge. I will have to really think about what I am reading to be sure that I understand it.*

The teacher skips to a riddle called "Strawberry Seeds."

> *One thing I have to remember to do is stop after I read a line or two to be sure that I understand the riddle. So, here we go!*
>
> > *"Strawberries grow along the ground,*
> >
> > *A better treat cannot be found!"*
>
> *I understand that. I have seen strawberry plants growing in a garden, and I love to eat them. They are a great treat.*
>
> > *"Their seeds reside in tiny rows,*
> >
> > *From each of them a plant will grow."*
>
> *I've seen strawberries and know that they have little seeds on the outside of the berry. I guess they grow in rows. I never really noticed how they were spread out on the berry. There is a picture that helps, though. Looking at the picture, I can see that the seeds are in rows, but there is not the same number of seeds in each row. It's not an array. I do know that plants grow from seeds. I wonder what the math riddle is? I'm pretty sure I understand the riddle so far.*
>
> > *"Just how many seeds are there?*
> >
> > *Count them only if you dare."*

Well, now I know what I need to find. I have to find out how many seeds there are to solve this riddle. I wonder why it says "count them if you dare?" Maybe if I read some more I will find out.

"Here's a little trick of mine:

Pair the rows that sum to nine!"

Oh—the author is giving me a hint about how to solve the riddle! He says to "pair the rows that sum to nine." I know that a pair is two of something—so I have to find rows in groups of two. Then—sum—that's what you get when you add numbers together. So, the number of seeds in the two rows that go together have to equal nine. I think I understand this riddle.

The top row has seven seeds, so I have to pair it with a row with two seeds—that's the bottom row. The next row has six, so I pair it with the row that has three. Then, the two middle rows go together: five and four equal nine.

Now, I have to find out how many seeds without counting them all. There are three pairs of rows with nine seeds in each pair. I can multiply: Three times nine equals 27. I think I have solved the riddle. I know why he said to "count them if you dare." There was a much easier way to find out how many. Reading on was a good fix-up strategy to use.

It helped me to stop after every two lines to be sure that I understood the riddle. If I had rushed through it, I might have missed some important information or been confused at the end. When you are working with mathematics, stop every so often and check to monitor your understanding. If you don't understand, you can try a fix-up strategy.

The teacher carefully described each step of the process of monitoring comprehension so that students were able to follow along. In addition, students were explicitly reminded that this is a strategy that they should use as they work with mathematics.

In another vignette, a teacher is reading *Shipwreck Detectives: Coordinate Planes* by Julia Wall (2009) to demonstrate how to use a text feature to assist in making meaning when reading.

> *Let's look at page 13 now.*

The teacher reads the first paragraph aloud.

> *It says that sea charts use a scale to show distance. I'm not sure what* scale *means, but the word is in bold print. I bet that means I can find it in a glossary. I am going to look at the back of the book to check the glossary.*

The teacher turns to the page, shown here.

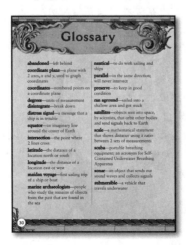

Scale *means a mathematical statement that shows distance using a ratio between two sets of measurements. Okay, so it is related to math and related to ratios. I know that ratios show how two things compare. This is talking about distance on a map. The map is not nearly the size of the area it represents. The next sentence talks about nautical miles. What are they?*

Nautical *is in the glossary, too. It means having to do with ships and sailing. I guess nautical miles are different from miles on land. I'm not sure—so I'm going to read further to see if it begins to make more sense to me.*

The teacher reads the next paragraph.

Ah! A nautical mile is longer than a land mile. It equals 1.15 land miles.

What does that have to do with scale? If someone is looking at a map and wants to see how far it is between two points, they would have to know the ratio between the distance on the map and the real distance. I get it—the scale tells that. I bet the map in my car uses a scale, too.

It is good that this book has a glossary and puts those words in bold print. That helped me understand what I was reading, and while the question was still on my mind. I was able to figure out the mathematics that I was confused about. If I had just skipped over that part, I wouldn't understand this part of the book. Always check to make sure you understand what you read. If not, think of fix-up strategies you can use to help you.

After seeing that students were ignoring the textual features that would increase comprehension, the teacher decided to model how to use the glossary, explicitly describing the thinking involved. The text was high interest, so students were already motivated to understand and were receptive to learning ways to monitor and improve their understanding. The teacher continued to observe students as they read to ensure that they monitored their own understanding and employed fix-up strategies when needed.

Chapter Snapshot

As students learn to monitor their mathematical understanding when working with mathematical ideas, reading mathematical texts, or working with problems, they are calling upon the full spectrum of comprehension strategies they have acquired. Depending upon their cognitive needs, they orchestrate the use of these tools to maximize their comprehension.

The metacognition of students, which is necessary to effectively use comprehension strategies, may begin with direct, explicit teacher explanations and modeling, but develops most fully with student practice. The value of this practice is enhanced when students have opportunities to explain their use of these strategies and share them with their peers (Pressley 2002). Unless students are aware when their understanding breaks down, they are unlikely to recognize their need for these strategies.

Mathematically proficient students monitor their thinking consistently and automatically as they ponder and work with mathematical ideas and problems. The key to their success is the intentional and conscious cultivation of the metacognitive skills to monitor understanding and reflect on mathematical concepts and problems. Students know when they encounter a comprehension roadblock; they possess the confidence and skill to rethink and switch strategies for a fresh start.

Review and Reflect

1. Monitoring comprehension encompasses the spectrum of comprehension strategies. It requires that students assume responsibility for their own understanding. In your classroom, what evidence would you look for to determine the degree to which students have assumed that role? What are some signs that might indicate that they need additional support?

2. How proficient are your students in regard to their metacognitive abilities? What can you do to strengthen their ability to monitor their mathematical comprehension?

Chapter 10

In the Guided Math Classroom

T his book has focused on ways in which comprehension strategies borrowed from literacy instruction can be adapted and used to enhance mathematics instruction. They are effective tools for building deep conceptual mathematical understanding in students. Although these thinking strategies may be integrated into any instructional approach, they mesh particularly well with the Guided Math instructional framework. To see why, one need only consider the foundational principles of a Guided Math classroom (Sammons 2009) (figure 10.1).

Fig. 10.1. The Foundational Principles of a Guided Math Classroom

- All children can learn mathematics.
- A numeracy-rich environment promotes mathematical learning by students.
- Learning at its best is a social process.
- Learning mathematics is a constructive process.
- An organized classroom environment supports the learning process.
- Modeling and think-alouds, combined with ample opportunities for guided and independent problem solving and purposeful conversations, create a learning environment in which students' mathematical understanding grows.
- Ultimately, children are responsible for their learning.

(Sammons 2009; adapted from Fountas and Pinnell 2001)

The Foundational Principles of a Guided Math Classroom

All children can learn mathematics.

Although No Child Left Behind brought this principle to the forefront, it is something that teachers *know*. It is our responsibility to see that all students are challenged. The National Mathematics Advisory Panel (2008) reports students' beliefs about learning are directly related to their performance in mathematics. Studies have shown that when they believe that their efforts to learn make them smarter, they are more persistent in pursuing their mathematics learning. Frequently, parents excuse their children's lack of achievement in mathematics as if it were an inherent ability that one either does or does not have. Along with challenging our students, we need to create an environment where students recognize the relationship between effort and learning.

Teaching students "turn-to" strategies to improve their understanding of new mathematical challenges reinforces the belief that effort and reflection result in better comprehension. Respect their ability to struggle through difficult, sometimes confusing, mathematical concepts and problems. Students learn that they bear the responsibility for making mathematical meaning. Teachers do not abdicate their roles, but instead they become facilitators working with students toward the ultimate goal of developing mathematicians.

A numeracy-rich environment promotes mathematical learning by students.

Borrowing from the research regarding literacy education, where immersion in a literacy-rich environment is considered essential to promote learning, it is important that children be immersed in a world of mathematics (Cambourne 1988). Mathematics is no longer solely problems in a textbook. As students see numbers and math-related materials throughout the classroom and participate in real-world, meaningful problem-solving opportunities, they begin to see the connection mathematics has to their own lives. This goes hand-in-hand with the comprehension strategies of making connections, inferring, and synthesizing. Mathematics begins to extend beyond the textbook and becomes something to ponder.

Learning at its best is a social process.

Vygotsky (1978) stressed the importance of children verbally expressing their ideas in the process of reasoning for themselves. They develop language through their experiences and begin to generalize their ideas through oral communication with a teacher or with fellow students. Reflective conversation and dialogue within a classroom setting is a tool that allows children to engage with the ideas of others and to construct hypotheses, strategies, and concepts (Nichols 2006). Learning is enhanced as students are at work with others exploring the same ideas (Van de Walle and Lovin 2006).

The meaning-making strategies explored in this text are conducive to communicating both verbal and written student thinking. Students working together to share their thinking and use of strategies is paramount in constructing mathematical meaning.

Learning mathematics is a constructive process.

As Fosnot and Dolk (2001) describe mathematical learning, "children learn to recognize, be intrigued by, and explore patterns, as they begin to overlay and interpret experiences, contexts, and phenomena with mathematical questions, tools (tables and charts), and models (the linear Unifix train versus the circular necklace). They are constructing an understanding of what it really means to be a mathematician—to organize and interpret their world through a mathematical lens. This is the essence of mathematics." The seven principles form a basis for this kind of mathematical learning.

An organized classroom environment supports the learning process.

Efficient organization of materials, use of time, and procedures established for students contribute to the effectiveness of the learning environment. Although the strategies are not directly related to this principle, an organized environment certainly supports their use by students. When students know the behavioral and learning expectations, they can use the comprehension strategies that support the construction of meaning.

Modeling and think-alouds, combined with ample opportunities for guided and independent problem solving and purposeful conversations, create a learning environment in which students' mathematical understanding grows.

Teachers set the stage for learning. By modeling problem-solving strategies that include multiple representations and approaches, students become aware that there is rarely only one correct way to approach problem solving. This risk-free environment, where mistakes are viewed as opportunities to learn, encourages students to investigate, recognize relationships, and begin to generalize from their experiences.

Effective teachers orchestrate instructional strategies based on the content, the needs of the class, and the needs of individual students, with the ultimate goal of supporting all students as they begin to understand mathematical "big ideas" and gain proficiency in organizing and interpreting the world through a mathematical lens (Fosnot and Dolk 2001). Independent student thinking and reflection on the meaning of the concepts and problems is inherent. The seven principles provide a structure of thinking that supports the understanding of "big ideas."

Ultimately, children are responsible for their learning.

As Marilyn Burns (2000) observed, "You cannot talk a child into learning or tell a child to understand." However, this does not absolve a teacher of responsibility. Educators establish the motivation and opportunity for students to learn. Cochran (1991) describes this principle: "And once, I had a teacher who understood. He brought with him the beauty of mathematics. He made me create it for myself. He gave me nothing, and it was more than any other teacher has ever dared to give me." Teaching students to think productively and reflectively, offering them the opportunities to explore mathematical ideas and build mathematical meaning through problems, and sharing with them the expectation that they can develop their knowledge of mathematics concepts, procedures, and practices, leads students to create for themselves the beauty of mathematics.

The Components of a Guided Math Classroom

Guided Math establishes a flexible instructional framework for teaching mathematics for the 21st century. It is designed to support teachers who find the traditional model of whole-class instruction does not meet the diverse instructional needs of their students. With the goal of building deep conceptual mathematics understanding and computational fluency, teachers who implement the Guided Math framework determine the unique needs of their students and then prescriptively address them using a combination of whole-class instruction, small-group instruction, math workshop, and conferences within a carefully designed classroom environment (Sammons 2009).

The specific instructional components of this model include:

1. A classroom environment of numeracy

2. Math Stretches and calendar board activities

3. Whole-class instruction

4. Guided Math instruction with small groups of students

5. Math workshop

6. Individual conferences

7. An ongoing system of assessment

Together, these components shown in figure 10.2 (on the next page) provide the format for implementing research-based best practices in classrooms and supporting the mathematical learning needs of all students.

Fig. 10.2. Guided Math: Daily Menu of Instruction

Daily: A Classroom Environment of Numeracy
Surround students with mathematics. This includes real-life math tasks, data analysis, math word walls, instruments of measurement, mathematical communication, class-created math charts, graphic organizers, calendars, and evidence of problem solving.

Daily: Math Stretches and Calendar Math
Prepare students for the "Your Choice" instruction to come with Math Stretches, calendar board activities, problems of the day, math-related classroom responsibilities, data work, incredible equations, review of skills to be maintained, and previews of skills to come.

Your Choice: Whole-Class Instruction
Use when students are working at the same level of achievement, to introduce lessons with a mini-lesson or activating strategy, to model and think-aloud, when reading aloud math-related literature, conducting a Math Huddle, reviewing previously mastered skills, setting the stage for Math Workshop, or for written assessments.

Your Choice: Small-Group Instruction
Change the composition of small groups based on students' needs. The differentiated instruction for these groups offers opportunities to introduce new concepts, practice new skills, work with manipulatives, provide intensive and targeted instruction to struggling learners, introduce activities that will later become part of Math Workshop, conduct informal assessments, and re-teach based on student needs.

Your Choice: Math Workshop
Students work independently individually, in pairs, or in cooperative groups. The work may be a follow-up to whole-class or small-group instruction, ongoing practice of previously mastered skills, investigations, math games, Math Journals, or interdisciplinary work.

Daily: Conferencing
To enhance learning, confer individually with students, informally assessing their understandings, providing opportunities for one-on-one mathematical communications, and determining teaching points for individual students as well as for the class.

Daily: Assessment
Include a generous helping of assessment *for* learning to inform instruction, with a dollop *of* assessment of learning to top off each unit.

(Sammons 2009)

A Classroom Environment of Numeracy

Environments rich in mathematical opportunities for children are essential if we want our children to develop a thorough understanding of mathematics. When students begin to recognize how numbers and problem solving affect their everyday lives, mathematics becomes more meaningful to them. Because learning is both a social and constructive process, the best way for children to learn to use and extend their number senses is through active engagement in authentic opportunities.

This setting is ideal for promoting the application of the comprehension strategies by students. The opportunity to be actively engaged in mathematical tasks challenges students to make sense of what they experience and observe. Lively discourse feeds the use of thinking strategies, prompting students to reflect, reassess their thinking, and revise their ideas when needed.

The creation of a classroom environment supporting numeracy enables students to build on their previously acquired understanding of numbers—thus, making connections to prior knowledge. An organized mathematical support system for students requires that we encourage children to use manipulatives, compute, compare, categorize, question, estimate, solve problems, converse, and write about their thinking processes. All of these activities spur student thinking and present opportunities to teach students to monitor their mathematical understanding and to apply fix-up strategies if they notice their comprehension wanes.

Providing a challenging and supportive classroom learning community is a requisite for rigorous mathematics instruction (NCTM 2000). In such a classroom, each student understands that he or she can and, indeed, is expected to engage in making meaning of the world mathematically (Fosnot and Dolk 2001). In this community, students are given opportunities to learn the "big ideas" of mathematics. They also participate in a supportive climate of inquiry where ideas are generated, expressed, and justified, thus creatively exploring mathematical relationships and constructing meaning. This setting requires students to have a tool box of comprehension strategies on which they can rely when building this understanding.

Math Stretches and Calendar Board Activities

In a classroom focused on mathematics, brief morning math activities serve as a "warm-up" and set the tone for the day. Having just arrived at school, children need time to shift gears from readying themselves for school, family conversations, rides on the school bus, and chats with friends as they walk to the classroom. So, as soon as the students complete their morning "housekeeping" chores, they are engaged in mini-math activities from a range of mathematical concepts. Some activities require students to review concepts already covered and mastered. Some relate to mathematical concepts currently explored. Some give students a preview or taste of concepts to be introduced or extended. Although these activities are short in duration, they are carefully planned, based on the standards taught and student needs.

A Math Stretch activity promotes mathematical thinking while students transition from the busyness of their morning routines to help them begin to think mathematically. These simple activities ask students to indicate their answers to a question on a class graph, table, or diagram. Once everyone has completed the daily stretch, the class gets together for a Math Huddle to discuss the results (Sammons 2009).

The Math Stretch task itself is one that requires thinking and impels students to consider what they already know relative to the assigned task. If students have been taught the seven foundation principles, they begin making connections, determining importance, making inferences or predictions, asking questions, visualizing—maybe even synthesizing. They are also continuously monitoring what they know and understand. In the student response section of the stretch, these strategies are used independently by learners.

During the Math Huddle that follows, their thinking is shared with others. Students are encouraged to be metacognitively active; their thinking should evolve as they engage in the discussion with their fellow students.

The calendar board provides a versatile vehicle for preview, practice, and maintenance of important grade-level skills. The consistency of daily instruction while using a calendar board helps students incrementally build understanding of mathematical "big ideas," challenges them to notice patterns and relationships, and encourages them to share mathematical insights with their classmates (Sammons 2009). These are valuable habits for students to develop.

Combine Math Stretches and calendar board activities to encourage students to practice using the comprehension strategies and to have students use new math vocabulary. These opportunities let students revisit mathematics concepts in a variety of contexts and, as a consequence, they develop a multifaceted and deep conceptual understanding.

Whole-Class Instruction

Whole-class instruction is a time when everyone receives the same information and engages in the same activity at the same time. Use it for mini-lessons, for modeling and think-alouds, or for activating strategies as you begin a new unit of study. It can also be a time for the class to come together as a mathematics community to share their thinking about complex mathematical issues—even primary students. The degree of complexity varies according to the cognitive sophistication of the learners.

During these mathematical conversations, students should be encouraged to share their thinking, not just their answers or solutions to problems. By examining ways of handling confusion and lack of understanding, students have opportunities to learn from each other and expand their repertoire of strategies.

Whole-class instruction does have drawbacks. Some students are hesitant to speak up in a large group. Others may become distracted or inattentive. There is rarely sufficient time for everyone in the class to participate as they do in a small-group setting. It is important to be aware of these limitations and use it selectively.

Guided Math Instruction with Small Groups of Students

Guided Math is best used during small-group instruction. Teachers assess students formally or informally, and then group them according to their proficiency at given skills (Sammons 2009) and according to their learning needs. The groups are homogeneous yet fluid and change as student needs change. Work with small groups of students with similar instructional needs to closely observe student work, monitor their attention, provide strong support for struggling learners, and provide extra challenges for more proficient learners.

By working with small groups, everyone is an active contributor to the mathematical discussions. It is easy to reliably assess students' abilities to apply the comprehension strategies. Carefully craft questions to guide students to explore ways of increasing their understanding of mathematical concepts and problems. When needed, model the use of these strategies, thinking aloud as necessary. In this more intimate setting, students who have trouble grasping a strategy in a large group often catch on quickly. If they do not, it is easy to recognize and to promptly provide additional instructional support.

Math Workshop

In Math Workshop, students assume full responsibility for tasks planned by the teacher. They work independently, individually, or in small groups. The procedures and expectations should be clear so students can carry out the assigned work without guidance, freeing the teacher to work with small groups and to confer without interruption.

It is during Math Workshop that students practice their comprehension strategies independently. Although the teacher certainly monitors their work and provides timely and specific feedback, students know that they are "flying solo" during this component of Guided Math.

Provide scaffolding such as prompts, anchor charts, or graphic organizers to remind students of the strategies they have learned or to help them organize their thinking. But, overall, this is a time when students have the chance to show what they know.

Individual Conferences

The Guided Math framework supports one-on-one conferences with students to assess their understanding of mathematical skills or concepts, to clarify or correct misunderstandings and errors, to extend or refine understanding, and to ensure their success (Sammons 2009). Use this time to monitor students' ability to apply mathematical comprehension strategies.

Conference with individual students at any time throughout the day. Meet briefly to further students' understanding of mathematical concepts. These brief conversations provide rich information about the instructional needs of individual students as well as help identify specific teaching points for the class as a whole.

Math conferences are especially useful in gently prodding students who may lack confidence to enter into a mathematical conversation. The scaffolding provided in these situations increases student confidence as they explain their ideas in nonthreatening one-on-one dialogues. Moreover, this intimate conversational setting allows you to guide student thinking and explore strategies to employ when understanding breaks down.

An Ongoing System of Assessment

How do you determine the instructional needs of students for the Guided Math framework? Ideally, a balanced system of assessment will give you a complete picture of each child's understanding, not just a single glimpse from a test.

Formative and summative assessments such as observations of students' work, discussions with students, and assessment of their finished products, all give valuable perspectives on their capabilities and needs. In addition, to maximize their own learning, students themselves must be involved in assessing their own work based on criteria, rubrics, or exemplars. To truly "leave no child behind," assessment should be more than just giving grades on tests and on report cards.

Assessing the ability to effectively use comprehension strategies relies on the teachers' communication with their students. Students can share their thinking either orally or in writing. Just as teachers give students a glimpse into their minds when they think-aloud, students must provide that same kind of insight for teachers if teachers are to accurately assess a student's ability.

Teaching Students to Become Mathematicians

Focus on what prepares and motivates a student to assume the role of a young mathematician. This does not mean simply working the next page in the textbook. Students respond when they are challenged; they rise to meet our expectations. Our expectations and the mathematical environments we create impact their visions of themselves in the world of mathematics. Students who are learning mathematics should (Sammons 2009):

- explore problem solving in a risk-free environment where errors are seen as learning opportunities

- try out strategies with a variety of challenging problems

- identify appropriate strategies to use when problem solving

- feel the satisfaction of struggling with difficult problems and then finally solving them

- receive specific feedback from teachers and peers on their mathematical work

- participate in mathematical conversations using mathematical vocabulary and justifying their work

- expand their mathematical understanding through problem-solving tasks and mathematical discourse

- learn to recognize patterns and relationships leading to the development of conjectures

- make mathematical connections

A common thread that runs through these attributes is the importance of providing students with experiences that instill in them the belief that thinking mathematically makes sense. And, through these experiences, students come to believe that they are capable of making sense of mathematics.

The belief of students that they can make sense of this complex discipline is paramount. Foster this belief by teaching students how to use strategies that carry them beyond simple computations, deep below the surface manifestations of mathematical applications, and into the realm of mathematical exploration. The comprehension strategies that have been so effective in literacy instruction give students the cognitive tools they need for making sense of mathematics and for moving from the role of mathematical technicians to that of true mathematicians.

The literacy-mathematics link envisioned by Arthur Hyde (2006) in *Comprehending Math: Adapting Reading Strategies to Teach Mathematics K–6* is one in which thinking, language, and mathematics are braided together into a "tightly knit entity like a rope that is stronger than the individual strands." The three components are inseparable, mutually supportive, and necessary. As such, many of the cognitive strategies that students must learn to apply are interdisciplinary—equally as valuable with literacy, mathematics, and analytic thinking.

In reading, students use discrete decoding skills, and construct meaning by interacting with the text. They draw upon their background knowledge as they infer and predict, make connections, ask questions, visualize, determine importance, and synthesize, combining the new information from the text with the old to construct meaning. In working with mathematics, encourage students to use the same strategies as they construct mathematical meaning.

As Hyde expands on the similarities between reading and mathematics comprehension strategies, he asks a set of questions derived from reading strategies for mathematics teachers to consider:

1. Are students expected to *construct their own meaning* in mathematics?

2. Are students encouraged to have *ownership of their problem solving*—to choose to use mathematics for purposes they set for themselves?

3. Are students encouraged to do problem solving for *authentic purposes?*

4. Are students encouraged to do *voluntary mathematics*, selecting tasks for information, pleasure, or to fulfill personal goals?

5. How is mathematics instruction *scaffolded?*

6. Does the school help teachers and students build a *rich, mathematically literate environment* or community?

7. Are students encouraged to see the *big picture, important concepts, and vital connections* versus isolated pieces of mathematics?

8. Is *forgiveness* granted to students in mathematics? Is making *mistakes a natural* part of learning? Is doing mathematics seen as a dynamic process that incorporates *planning, drafting, revising, editing, and publishing?*

These are worth considering when implementing Guided Math and applying literacy strategies. It helps to have support during a time of change. Joining together in learning communities makes the process easier and more effective. Working together, teachers examine and reflect on their teaching practices. They plan, teach, share, and refine. This collaboration leads to growth for the entire group. As a consequence, the students of these teachers benefit from this growth.

Faced with increased accountability, it is easy to lose sight of the ultimate goal of education. We know what we want for our students: to inspire them to be interested, curious, inventive, and capable of rigorous thinking. When we plan for instruction, however, the pressure to "teach to the test" is always in the back of our minds.

Teachers shoulder the enormous responsibility of working within the guidelines of their school systems to establish learning environments in which their students become young mathematicians. Late at night, many of them lie awake and wonder whether they are providing the best learning experiences for their charges. Can their students learn and be able to prove it on the state-mandated tests?

It may help to step back and put the study of mathematics in perspective. Each year of mathematical learning builds a foundation for the mathematics that students use during their lifetime. What might appear to be a shortcut to success on a standardized test may hamper students in the future. When teachers immerse their students in the exploration of mathematics, inspire in them a sense of wonder and curiosity, support their thinking by teaching them how to apply comprehension strategies, and establish mathematical communities in their classrooms, students begin to develop a deep understanding of mathematical concepts that they will retain and be able to apply to real-life problems. There are no shortcuts.

Chapter Snapshot

Teaching students to use comprehension strategies enhances classroom mathematics instruction, whether or not teachers implement the Guided Math framework. For teachers who do use the Guided Math approach, these strategies mesh particularly well with both its foundational principles and individual components. They may be taught and practiced by students throughout the instructional modes that comprise the framework.

As teachers encourage their students to think of themselves as mathematicians and see the discipline as one that makes sense, students need a variety of tools to make meaning when they encounter mathematical challenges. Explicitly teaching students how to apply these comprehension strategies provides them with these tools. It gives students confidence that they can make sense of this complex subject, thus moving them from being mathematical technicians to being true mathematicians.

Review and Reflect

1. Reflect on the instructional framework you use for teaching mathematics. What are its strengths? In what areas would you like to improve?

2. How can you integrate the use of the vocabulary and comprehension strategies into your daily mathematics instruction? What might you try first?

Frayer Diagram

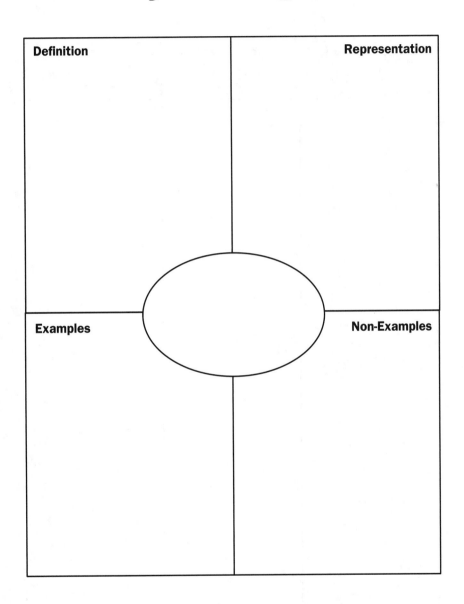

| Definition | Representation |
| Examples | Non-Examples |

Math Connections

My Connections	Important to Me	Important to Understanding the Math

Question Journal

Question	Before, During, or After?	Predicted Answer	Final Answer

Multiple Representations Graphic Organizer

Mathematical Symbols	Real-Life Example

Model or Diagram	Explain with Words

Inference and Evidence Chart

Inference	Evidence

Comprehension Checklist

1. Get ready to think mathematically
- ❏ scan texts for illustrations, diagrams, and text features
- ❏ consider your purpose for the mathematical work
- ❏ reflect on what you already know about the concept or problem

2. Monitor your comprehension as you work
- ❏ notice what you do not understand
- ❏ apply fix-up strategies

3. Improve your comprehension as you work
- ❏ make connections
- ❏ ask questions
- ❏ visualize
- ❏ make inferences or predictions
- ❏ determine what is important
- ❏ synthesize

4. Check your comprehension again as you complete your work
- ❏ explain your understanding in your own words
- ❏ check that your solution makes sense

Comprehension Constructor

I am confused by:

_____

This is what I am thinking:

_____

I will try this fix-up strategy:

_____

Now I understand:

_____

I am still confused and need some help to understand:

_____

_____

_____

_____

_____

References Cited

Baldi, S., Y. Jin, M. Skemer, P. J. Green, D. Herget, and H. Xie. 2007. *Highlights from PISA 2006: Performance of U.S. 15 year-old students in science and mathematics literacy in an international context*. Washington, DC: National Center for Educational Statistics, Institute of Education Sciences, United States Department of Education, http://nces.ed.gov/pubs2008/2008016_1.pdf

Bamberger, H. J. and C. Oberdorf. 2007. *Introduction to connections: Grades 3–5*. The Math Process Standards Series. Portsmouth, NH: Heinemann.

Bamberger, H. J., C. Oberdorf, and K. Schultz-Ferrell. 2010. *Math misconceptions: From misunderstanding to deep understanding*. Portsmouth, NH: Heinemann.

Beck, I. L., M. G. McKeown, and L. Kucan. 2002. *Bringing words to life: Robust vocabulary instruction*. New York, NY: Guilford Press.

Bill, V. L. and I. Jamar. 2010. Disciplinary literacy in the mathematics classroom. In *Content matters: A disciplinary literacy approach to improving student learning,* ed. S. McConachie and A. Petrosky, Kindle edition. 1405–1862. San Francisco, CA: Jossey-Bass.

Block, C. C. and M. Pressley. 2007. *Best practices in teaching comprehension*. In *Best practices in literacy instruction,* 3rd ed., ed. L.B. Gambrell, L.M. Morrow, and M. Pressley, eds. Kindle edition. 2902–3202. London: Guilford Press.

Block, P. 2001. *The answer to how is yes: Acting on what matters*. San Francisco: Berrett-Koehler.

Boaler, J. 2008. *What's math got to do with it? Helping children learn to love their most hated subject—And why it's important for America*. New York: Viking.

Brassell, D. and T. Rasinski. 2008. *Comprehension that works: Taking students beyond ordinary understanding to deep comprehension*. Huntington Beach, CA: Shell Education.

Brummer, T. and S. Macceca. 2008. *Reading strategies for mathematics*. Huntington Beach, CA: Shell Education.

Bruner, R. F. 2001 Repetition is the first principle of all learning. Available at *Social Science Research Network,* August 16, 2001, http://ssrn.com/abstract=224340.

Burns, M. 2010. Snapshots of student misunderstandings. *Educational Leadership* 67 (6): 18–22.

Burns, M. 2000. *About teaching mathematics: A K–8 resource*. Sausalito, CA: Math Solutions Publication.

Calkins, L. 2000. *The art of teaching reading*. Boston, MA: Allyn and Bacon.

——— 1994. *The art of teaching writing*. Portsmouth, NH: Heinemann.

Cambourne, B. 1988. *The whole story: Natural learning and the acquisition of literacy in the classroom.* New York, NY: Ashton Scholastic.

Carpenter, T., M. Franke, and L. Levi. 2003. *Thinking mathematically: Integrating arithmetic and algebra in elementary school.* Portsmouth, NH: Heinemann.

Chapin, S.H., C. O'Connor, and N.C. Anderson. 2003. *Classroom discussions: Using math talk to help students learn, grades 1–6.* Sausalito, CA: Math Solutions.

Cobb, P., M. Gresalfi, and L. L. Hodge. 2009. An interpretive scheme for analyzing the identities that students develop in mathematics classrooms. *Journal for Research in Mathematics.* 40 (January): 40–68.

Cochran, L. 1991. The art of the universe. *Journal of Mathematical Behavior* 10:213–214. Quoted in Van de Walle and Lovein 2006, ix.

Cohen, P. 2010. Digital keys for unlocking the humanities' riches. *New York Times*, November 17, 2010, http://www.nytimes.com/2010/11/17/arts/17digital.html (accessed November 17, 2010).

Common Core State Standards Initiative. Common core state standards: Mathematics. http://www.corestandards.org/the-standards/mathematics.

Duffy, G. G. 2003. *Explaining reading: A resource for teaching concepts, skills, and strategies.* New York, NY: Guilford Press.

Duke, N. K. and P. D. Pearson. 2002. Effective practices for developing reading comprehension. In *What research has to say about reading instruction.* 3rd ed. Eds. A. E. Farstup and S. J. Samuels, 202–242. Newark, DE: International Reading Association.

Dunlap, C. Z. and E. M. Weisman. 2006. *Helping English language learners succeed.* Huntington Beach, CA: Shell Education.

English, L. D. 2004. Mathematical and analogical reasoning in early childhood. *Mathematical and analogical reasoning of young learners.* Ed. L.D. English, 1–22. Mahwah, NJ: Lawrence Erlbaum Associates.

Fillingim, J. G. and A. T. Barlow. 2010. From the inside out. *Teaching children mathematics* 17 (2): 81–88.

Fleischman, H. L., P. J. Hopstock, M. P. Pelczar, and B. E. Shelley. 2010. *Highlights from PISA 2009: Performance of U.S. fifteen-year-old students in reading, mathematics, and science literacy in an international context* (NCES 2011-004). U.S. Department of Education, National Center for Education Statistics. Washington, D.C.: U.S. Government Printing Office. http://nces.ed.gov/pubs2011/2011004.pdf

Fosnot, C. and M. Dolk. 2001. *Young mathematicians at work: Constructing number sense, addition, and subtraction.* Portsmouth, NH: Heinemann.

Fountas, I., and G. Pinnell. 2001. *Guiding readers and writers grades 3–6.* Portsmouth, NH: Heinemann.

———. 1996. *Guided reading: Good first teaching for all children.* Portsmouth, NH: Heinemann.

Gerofsky, S. 2004. *A man left Albuquerque heading east: Word problems as genre in mathematics education.* New York, NY: Peter Lang.

Hart, B. and Risley, T. R. 1995. *Meaningful differences in the everyday experience of young American children.* Baltimore, MD: Brookes Publishing.

Harvey, S. and A. Goudvis. 2000. *Strategies that work: Teaching comprehension to enhance understanding.* York, ME: Stenhouse.

Harvey, S. and A. Goudvis. 2007. *Strategies that work: Teaching comprehension to enhance understanding.* 2nd ed. York, ME: Stenhouse.

Hibbing, A. N. and J. L. Rankin-Erickson. 2009. A picture is worth a thousand words: Using visual images to improve comprehension for middle school struggling readers. In *Essential readings on comprehension.* Eds. D. Lapp and D. Fisher, 32–47. Newark, DE: International Reading Association.

Hiebert, J., T. P. Carpenter, E. Fennema, K. Fuson, D. Wearne, H. Murray, A. Oliver, and P. Human. 1997. *Making sense: Teaching and learning mathematics with understanding.* Portsmouth, NH: Heinemann.

Hyde, A. 2006. *Comprehending math: Adapting reading strategies to teach mathematics, K–6.* Portsmouth, NH: Heinemann.

Keene, E. O. and S. Zimmermann. 1997. *Mosaic of thought: Teaching comprehension in a reader's workshop.* Portsmouth, NH: Heinemann.

———. 2007. *Mosaic of thought: The power of comprehension strategy instruction.* 2nd ed. Portsmouth, NH: Heinemann.

Kenney, J., E. Hancewicz, L. Heuer, D. Metsisto, and C. L. Tuttle. 2005. *Literacy strategies for improving mathematics instruction.* Alexandria, VA: Association for Supervision and Curriculum Development.

Kujawa, S. and L. Huske. 1995. *The strategic teaching and reading project guidebook.* Rev. ed. Oak Brook, IL: North Central Regional Educational Laboratory. (Quoted in T. Brummer and S. Macceca. 2008. *Reading strategies for mathematics.* Huntington Beach, CA: Shell Education.)

Lehr, F., J. Osborn, and E. H. Hiebert. 2004. *A focus on vocabulary.* Research-Based Practices in Early Reading Series 2. Honolulu, HI: Regional Education Laboratory at Pacific Resources for Education and Learning.

Marzano, R. J. 2004. *Building background knowledge for academic achievement: Research on what works in schools.* Alexandria, VA: Association for Supervision and Curriculum Development.

— 2007. *The art and science of teaching: A comprehensive framework for effective instruction.* Alexandria, VA: Association for Supervision and Curriculum Development.

Marzano, R. J. and D. J. Pickering. 2005. *Building academic vocabulary: Teacher's manual.* Alexandria, VA: Association for Supervision and Curriculum Development.

McGregor, T. 2007. *Comprehension connections: Bridges to strategic reading.* Portsmouth, NH: Heinemann.

McKenna, M. Vocabulary: Defining best practices in Reading First schools (PowerPoint)®, http://curry.edschool.virginia.edu/reading/projects/garf/ PowerPoints/VocabularyRF.ppt (accessed September 26, 2010).

——. 2004. Teaching vocabulary to struggling older readers. *Perspectives* 30(1):13–16.

McMillan, D. 2008. *Collecting data.* Huntington Beach, CA: Teacher Created Materials.

——. 2008. *Reading the newspaper: Estimating with multidigit numbers.* Huntington Beach, CA: Teacher Created Materials.

Miller, D. 2002. *Reading with meaning: Teaching comprehension in the primary grades.* Portland, ME: Stenhouse.

Mink, D. 2010. *Strategies for teaching mathematics.* Huntington Beach, CA: Shell Education.

Minton, L. 2007. *What if your ABC's were your 123's?: Building connections between literacy and numeracy.* Thousand Oaks, CA: Corwin Press.

Murphy, D. 2010. *You can't just say it louder! Differentiated strategies for comprehending nonfiction.* Huntington Beach, CA: Shell Education.

Murray, M. 2004. *Teaching mathematics vocabulary in context: Windows, doors, and secret passages.* Portsmouth, NH: Heinemann.

National Center for Education Statistics. Institute of Education Sciences. U.S. Department of Education. *Trends in international mathematics and science study.* http://nces.ed.gov/ timss/results07_math07.asp (accessed September 4, 2010).

National Council of Teachers of Mathematics. 2000. *Principles and standards for school mathematics.* Reston, VA: National Council of Teachers of Mathematics.

National Governors Association for Best Practices (NGABS) and Council of Chief State School Officers (CCSSO). 2010. *Common core state standards.* http://corestandards.org/ the-standards/mathematics (accessed November 19, 2010).

National Reading Panel. 2000. *Teaching children to read: An evidence-based assessment of the scientific research literature on reading and its implications for reading instruction.* Washington, DC: National Institute of Child Health and Human Development, National Institute of Health. http://www.nichd.nih.gov/publications/nrp/upload/smallbook_pdf.

National Research Council. 2001. *Adding it up: Helping children learn mathematics.* Ed. J. Kilpatrick, J. Swafford, and B. Findell. Mathematics Learning Study Committee, Center for Education, Division of Behavioral and Social Sciences and Education. Washington, DC: National Academy Press.

Nichols, M. 2006. *Comprehension through conversation: The power of purposeful talk in the reading workshop.* Portsmouth, NH: Heinemann.

O'Connell, S. 2007. *Now I get it: Strategies for building confident and competent mathematicians, K–6.* Portsmouth, NH: Heinemann.

——. 2007. *Introduction to problem solving.* The Math Process Standards Series. Portsmouth, NH: Heinemann.

Organisation for Economic Co-operation and Development. 2006. *Assessing scientific, reading and mathematical literacy: A framework for PISA 2006.* Paris: Author. http://www.oecd.org/dataoecd/63/35/37464175.pdf.

Owocki, G. 2003. *Comprehension: Strategic instruction for K–3 students.* Portsmouth, NH: Heinemann.

Pearson, P. and Gallagher, M. 1983. The instruction of reading comprehension. *Contemporary Educational Psychology* 8:317–344.

Pearson, P. D., L. R. Roehler, J. A. Dole, and G. G. Duffy. 1992. *Developing expertise in reading comprehension: What should be taught and how should it be taught?* In *What research has to say about reading instruction*, ed. J. Samuels and A. Farstrup, 145–199. 2nd ed. Newark, DE: International Reading Association.

Pólya, G. 1957. *How to solve it: A new aspect of mathematical method.* 2nd ed. Princeton, NJ: Princeton University Press.

Postman, N. 1995. *The end of education: Redefining the value of school.* New York, NY: Vintage Books.

Pressley, M. 2002. Metacognition and self-regulated comprehension. In *What research has to say about reading instruction*, ed. J. Samuels and A. Farstrup, 291–309. 3rd ed. Newark, DE: International Reading Association.

Raphael, T. 1982. Question answering strategies for students. *Reading Teacher.* 36(2): 186–190.

Riccomini, P. J. and B. S. Witzel. 2009. *Response to intervention in math.* Thousand Oaks, CA: Corwin.

Routman, R. 2003. *Reading essential: The specifics you need to teach reading well.* Portsmouth, NH: Heinemann.

Sadowski, M. 2005. A dual coding view of vocabulary learning. *Reading and Writing Quarterly.* 21(3): 221–238.

Sammons, L. 2009. *Guided math: A framework for mathematics instruction.* Huntington Beach, CA: Shell Education.

Sammons, L. 2010. *Math stretches: Building conceptual understanding (Grades K–2).* Huntington Beach, CA: Shell Education.

Sammons, L. 2010. *Math stretches: Building conceptual understanding (Grades 3–5).* Huntington Beach, CA: Shell Education.

Stahl, S. A., and Nagy, W. E. 2005. *Teaching word meanings.* Mahwah, NJ: Lawrence Erlbaum.

Taylor, B. T., L. Harris, P. D. Pearson, and G. E. Garcia. 1994. *Reading difficulties: Instruction and assessment.* 2nd ed. New York, NY: McGraw Hill.

Thompson, D. R., G. Kersaint, J. C. Richards, P. D. Hunsader, and R. N. Rubenstein. 2008. *Mathematical literacy: Helping students make meaning in the middle grades.* Portsmouth, NH: Heinemann.

Thompson, M. and J. Thomason. 2005. *Learning-focused schools strategies notebook.* Boone, NC: Learning Concepts, Inc.

Tovani, C. 2000. *I read it, but I don't get it: Comprehension strategies for adolescent readers.* Portland, ME: Stenhouse.

U.S. Department of Education. 2008. *The final report of the National Mathematics Advisory Panel.* Report of the National Mathematics Advisory Panel. http://www.ed.gov/MathPanel.

Van de Walle, J. and L. Lovin. 2006. *Teaching student-centered mathematics*, 2 vols. Boston, MA: Pearson.

Van de Walle, J., K. S. Karp, and J. M. Bay-Williams. 2010. *Elementary and middle school mathematics: Teaching developmentally.* 7th ed. Boston, MA: Allyn and Bacon.

Vygotsky, L. S. 1978. *Mind in society: The development of higher psychological processes.* Cambridge, MA: Harvard University Press.

Wagner, T. 2008. *The global achievement gap: Why even our best schools don't teach the new survival skills our children need—And what we can do about it.* New York, NY: Basic Books.

Walmsley, S. 2009. Getting the big idea: A neglected goal for reading comprehension. In *Essential readings on comprehension*, ed. D. Lapp and D. Fisher, 48–51. Newark, DE: International Reading Association.

Whitin, D. J. and P. E. Whitin. 2011. *Learning to read the numbers: Integrating critical literacy and critical numeracy in K–8 classrooms.* New York, NY: Routledge and Urbana, IL: National Council of Teachers of English.

Wilhelm, J. K. 2001. *Improving comprehension with think-aloud strategies: Modeling what good readers do.* New York, NY: Scholastic.

———. 2004. *Reading is seeing: Learning to visualize scenes, characters, ideas, and text worlds to improve comprehension and reflective reading.* New York, NY: Scholastic.

Children's Literature

Aker, Suzanne. *What comes in 2's, 3's, & 4's?* New York, NY: Simon and Schuster Books for Young Readers. 1990.

Bailey, L. *Stanley's party*. Tonawanda, NY: Kids Can Press, 2004.

Clement, R. *Counting on Frank*. Milwaukee, WI: Gareth Stevens, 1991.

Dahl, R. *Matilda*. New York, NY: Puffin, 2007.

Fromental, J. and J. Jolivet. *365 penguins*. New York, NY: Abrams Books for Young Readers, 2006.

Gelb, M. J. *How to think like Leonardo da Vinci: Seven steps to genius every day*. New York, NY: Dell, 1998.

Pilegard, V. *The warlord's alarm*. Gretna, LA: Pelican Publishing, 2006.

Rey, H. A. and M. Rey. *Curious George and the hot air balloon*. Boston, MA: Houghton Mifflin, 1998.

Scieszka, J. and Smith, L. *Math curse*. New York, NY: Viking, 1995.

Scriven, R.C. The Marrog. In *I like this poem: A classic anthology to treasure,* ed. K. Webb, 85. New York, NY: Penguin, 1979.

Slobodkina, E. *Caps for sale: A tale of a peddler, some monkeys and their monkey business*. New York, NY: Scholastic, 1940.

Speed, T. *Too cool cows*. New York, NY: The Putnam and Grosset Group, 1995.

Tang, G. *The grapes of math: Mind-stretching math riddles*. New York, NY: Scholastic, 2001.

Tompert, A. *Grandfather Tang's story*. New York, NY: Random House, 1990.

Wall, J. *Basketball angles: Understanding angles*. Huntington Beach, CA: Teacher Created Materials, 2009.

———. *Shipwreck detectives: Coordinate planes*. Huntington Beach, CA: Teacher Created Materials, 2009.